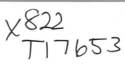

Shakespearean and Jacobean Tragedy

Rex Gibson

Series Editor: Adrian Barlow

CAMBRIDGE PRESS

PUBLISHED BY THE PRESS SYNDICATE OF THE UNIVERSITY OF CAMBRIDGE
The Pitt Building, Trumpington Street, Cambridge, United Kingdom

CAMBRIDGE UNIVERSITY PRESS
The Edinburgh Building, Cambridge CB2 2RU, UK
40 West 20th Street, New York, NY 10011- 4211, USA
10 Stamford Road, Oakleigh, VIC 3166, Australia
Ruiz de Alarcón 13, 28014 Madrid, Spain
Dock House, The Waterfront, Cape Town 8001, South Africa

http://www.cambridge.org

First published 2000

Printed in the United Kingdom at the University Press, Cambridge

Typefaces: Clearface and Mixage   *System:* QuarkXPress® 4.1

A catalogue record for this book is available from the British Library

ISBN 0 521 79562 1 paperback

Prepared for publication by Gill Stacey
Designed by Tattersall Hammarling & Silk
Cover photograph from the National Theatre's 1969 production of *The White
Devil* with Derek Godfrey, Geraldine McEwan and Edward Woodward. © Zoë
Dominic.

Contents

Introduction

Around 400 years ago, dazzling developments took place in English drama. In the closing years of the reign of Queen Elizabeth I, and throughout the reign of King James I (the Jacobean period), Shakespeare and his fellow playwrights wrote plays which thrilled packed audiences in London's booming theatres. Many of those plays have successfully stood the test of time and are still performed and enjoyed today. This book is concerned with one particular genre from that period: Shakespearean and Jacobean tragedy.

As you will discover, it was no accident that tragedy flowered so brilliantly between 1590 and 1625. The violence and suffering portrayed in the tragedies struck responsive chords in contemporary audiences. This book describes the social, cultural and historical contexts in which the plays were written. It shows how the tragedies of Shakespeare and the Jacobean playwrights were influenced by, and reflected, the troubled conditions of their times.

Those troubles took many forms. Beneath the glittering surface of the courts of Elizabeth and James, corruption flourished. Both monarchs lived in constant fear of assassination. Beyond the court, the huge gap between rich and poor was a powerful source of social unrest. Women lacked rights and were considered subordinate and inferior to men. For the great majority of the population, disease and violence, suffering and death were part of everyday experience. Public executions attracted larger crowds than any theatre audience. This was a disturbed society, very unlike the 'Merrie England' of popular myth.

Tragedies echoed the brutalities and injustices of the times, and mirrored other features of the age. England was a society in the process of change. Exploration was opening up new worlds, the discoveries of science were rapidly expanding knowledge, and the country was fiercely divided in matters of religion. Old certainties were questioned, and individuals increasingly found themselves in conflict with political or religious authority.

These anxious, sceptical times fuelled the imagination of Shakespeare and other playwrights. Their tragedies enabled Elizabethans and Jacobeans to scrutinise themselves and their society. But tragedy is also rooted in abiding concerns and emotions common to human beings in all ages. Tragedy shows how characters cope, or fail to cope with destructive impulses. It dramatically portrays how the desire for revenge is balanced with conflicting impulses of mercy, justice and forgiveness. In tragedy, individuals strive for a sense of self-worth as they struggle in defence of family, honour, social bonds, or personal identity. In short, tragedy explores what it is to be human, and this book invites you to consider how the tragedies of Shakespeare and the Jacobeans are still fresh and relevant today.

How this book is organised

Part 1: Tragedy
Part 1 discusses the nature of tragedy and gives a first introduction to Shakespearean and Jacobean tragedy.

Part 2: Contexts
Part 2 identifies the cultural, social and historical contexts of Shakespearean and Jacobean tragedy.

Part 3: Approaching the texts
Part 3 examines how particular tragedies reflect, or are influenced by, the times at which they were written and staged.

Part 4: Extracts from the tragedies
Part 4 contains extracts from the tragedies discussed in this book, or used as the focus for tasks and assignments.

Part 5: Critical approaches
Part 5 discusses the different ways in which critics have written about Shakespearean and Jacobean tragedy, and examines the nature of contemporary critical approaches.

Part 6: How to write about Shakespearean and Jacobean tragedy
Part 6 offers guidelines and assignments for those for whom this book is chiefly intended: students covering the topic as part of an advanced course in literary studies.

Part 7: Resources
This part contains a chronology, together with guidance on further reading, and a glossary and index.

At different points throughout the book, and at the end of Parts 1, 2, 3, 5 and 6 there are tasks and assignments, designed to help the reader reflect on ideas discussed in the text.

All extracts and quotations are taken from the New Cambridge Shakespeare series or have been specially edited for this book.

1 | Tragedy

- What is tragedy?

- What is Shakespearean tragedy?

- What is Jacobean tragedy?

- What were the origins of tragedy?

What is tragedy?

What do you understand by 'tragedy'? Consider the following three sentences which show how 'tragedy' is used today:

'Thousands were killed by the earthquake; it was a tragedy.'

'We lost the match; it's a tragedy.'

'Shakespeare's *Hamlet* is a tragedy.'

The first example shows the major meaning of 'tragedy'. It is a disaster or dreadful calamity in real life; a fatal event or series of events that causes suffering and grief. When people are killed in an earthquake or in some other catastrophe, no one doubts that a tragedy has happened.

The second example ('We lost the match') illustrates how 'tragedy' is often used in everyday speech to describe any mishap or upset, however minor. But losing a sports match is not something that most people consider utterly disastrous. The fans and the players involved are certainly disappointed at losing, but compared with the loss of life in an earthquake or other disaster, the difference in the use of 'tragedy' is obvious.

The third example reveals the meaning of 'tragedy' that is the concern of this book. Saying that *Hamlet* is a tragedy means that it is a particular kind of play, written in a distinctive style, and following certain conventions about characters, events and other matters. So tragedy is a **genre** of literature. What are the defining features of that genre? A first definition is that tragedies are plays which portray human suffering, and which end in disaster or death. Tragedies typically show the fall of a great hero (where 'hero' simply means the main character), presenting the troubles that afflict a great man or woman and result in his or her death.

But throughout this book you will be urged to criticise all such definitions. You will be invited to evaluate them against what they claim to describe, and to make your own judgements about their helpfulness. As you read on you will find plenty of material that will enable you to question, expand, and refine the definition of tragedy given in the preceding paragraph.

▶ What is your own definition of 'tragedy'? Give some actual examples of events or plays or films, and say why you consider them to be tragic.

What is Shakespearean tragedy?

When Shakespeare's plays were first published as a collection in 1623 (the First Folio), the contents page grouped the plays under three genre headings: Comedies, Histories, Tragedies. For the past 200 years, scholars have argued over those classifications, and have created others. For each play they have asked the same question: 'What kind of play is this?', and they have suggested additional categories to group the plays, for example, 'tragi-comedies', 'problem plays', 'late plays', 'romances'.

The problem of classifying the plays is evident by simply considering *Richard III*, which in Shakespeare's time was titled *The Tragedy of Richard the Third*. It is obviously a history, but it has a great deal of humour in it, and it has tragic features: there is much suffering, and the 'hero' is killed at the end. But for all the problems of classification, certain claims can be made with confidence. Virtually all Shakespeare scholars agree that Shakespeare wrote five supreme tragedies: *Hamlet*, *Othello*, *King Lear*, *Macbeth*, *Antony and Cleopatra*. They also agree that a number of his other plays can be regarded as tragedies, because they contain many features of the genre of tragedy.

It is also clear that Shakespeare himself was very well aware of the conventions of tragedy and what an audience would expect to see and hear when watching a tragedy at the Globe, where many of his plays were performed. He sometimes refers to 'tragedy' in his plays, often mockingly. In *A Midsummer Night's Dream*, the mechanicals are laughed at by the court for their 'merry and tragical' performance of *Pyramus and Thisbe*. In *Hamlet*, Shakespeare uses Polonius to ridicule the whole scholarly business of classifying plays. Polonius tells of the arrival of the actors at Elsinore:

> The best actors in the world, either for tragedy, comedy, history, pastoral, pastoral-comical, historical-pastoral, tragical-historical, tragical-comical-historical-pastoral …

'Shakespearean tragedy' refers to a number of very different plays sharing certain common features. They are about high status persons who increasingly suffer as the play progresses, and who die at the end. They are set in places remote in place and/or time, but the emotions the characters experience are still utterly familiar today. They are 'political' in the sense that what happens to the main characters affects the society in which they live. As you read on, you will discover other features which will help your understanding of tragedy.

▶ What follows are very brief summaries of those plays that scholars today generally agree to be Shakespeare's tragedies. They are in the order that Shakespeare probably wrote them, beginning with the earliest. To gain a first impression of their range and variety, find a way of presenting your understanding of 'Shakespearean tragedy'. You might for example work in a small group and rehearse and present a three-minute playlet: a very active 'show', parodying the twelve plays, using the brief descriptions as a 'script'. Or you may prefer to work alone or in pairs and design a list, illustration, or diagram to show the links, similarities or contrasts (for example, 'where?' [place]; 'when' [time]; 'who?' ['hero'/status], etc.).

Titus Andronicus: Titus, a loyal general of Ancient Rome, is driven by a rigid code of honour. He kills his own son, finds his daughter raped and mutilated, and is progressively tormented by his enemies. He endures grief and madness. Shortly before he is killed, he cooks his daughter's violators and serves them in a pie to their mother.

Romeo and Juliet: The two lovers enjoy only brief happiness together before the mutual hatred of their families parts them and sets them on the road to death in the Capulet tomb.

Richard III: Richard ambitiously plots and murders his way to the throne of England. But he does not enjoy quiet possession of the crown. Tormented by the ghosts of those he has murdered, he is killed at the battle of Bosworth.

Richard II: Richard arrogantly misuses his kingly powers. Threatened and finally overthrown by his cousin, Bullingbrook, he is increasingly racked with anxieties and shifting moods. He is murdered in his prison cell.

Julius Caesar: Brutus, not Caesar, is probably the tragic 'hero'. Caesar is killed before the play has reached its mid-point. Brutus, one of his assassins, flees Rome, fights a final battle, and stoically endures defeat and death.

Hamlet: Urged by his father's ghost to avenge his murder, Hamlet, Prince of Denmark, delays taking revenge. He is troubled by his conscience and his relationships with other characters. Hamlet's final acceptance of the need to act results in his death.

Othello: Othello is a great general in the service of Venice. His ensign, the malevolent Iago, persuades him that his wife is unfaithful. Othello is driven to the extremes of jealousy and moral disintegration. He murders his innocent wife, learns the truth of Iago's deception, and commits suicide.

King Lear: Lear angrily rejects his honest daughter Cordelia, but is cruelly mistreated by his other two daughters to whom he has given his kingdom. He goes mad, recovers, is reunited with Cordelia, only to see her murdered. He dies, but whether in despair or hope, Shakespeare leaves the audience to decide.

Timon of Athens: Timon, a wealthy nobleman, entertains with extravagant generosity. He becomes bankrupt, his former 'friends' refuse to help him, and he withdraws into obsessive misanthropy (hatred of humankind) and a lonely death.

Macbeth: Three witches predict that Macbeth, a victorious general, will become king. Prompted by his wife, he murders King Duncan and rules Scotland as a tyrant. But his imagination and conscience torment him, and although he fights bravely he is killed in a final battle.

Antony and Cleopatra: Set in Egypt and Rome, the play shows how love brings low the once great Antony. He fights his previous allies, is defeated, fumbles his suicide, but dies in Cleopatra's arms. She too chooses suicide, and dies in magnificent state rather than endure humiliation in Rome.

Coriolanus: Coriolanus is a brilliantly successful war leader, but a hopeless politician in peace. His pride and his contempt for the working class of Rome cause his exile. He joins his former enemies the Volsces to destroy Rome, but his love for his mother makes him abandon the attempt, and he is killed by the Volsces.

What is Jacobean tragedy?

'Jacobean tragedy' refers to tragedies written during the reign of King James I from 1603–1625. Those years are called the Jacobean period because *Jacobus* is Latin for James. Like 'Shakespearean tragedy', 'Jacobean tragedy' (sometimes called **'revenge tragedy'** or 'the theatre of blood') identifies a genre: plays which share certain distinctive features. What follows is a first account of the major characteristics of Jacobean tragedy. As you work through this book you can deepen your understanding by adding to this preliminary description.

* Revenge
  A character plans revenge for a wrong committed. Sometimes many characters seek revenge, and the play charts how the various quests for vengeance result in violent deaths. Different attitudes to revenge are explored, for example as a sacred duty of honour, or as an offence against both God and civil society. Disguise, plots and counterplots are common as revengers seek to achieve vengeance.

* Brutal and wicked behaviour
  The plays portray unpleasant and vicious aspects of humanity. Murder, treachery and cruelty frequently occur. Sexual lust and the desire for power and possessions are major motives for action, but such appetites lead to destruction and self-destruction. An atmosphere of moral and spiritual decay pervades the plays.

- The corrupt society of Renaissance Italy and Spain
  The plays are usually set in a decadent and vice-ridden foreign court, full of self-seekers and **machiavellian** political intrigue (crafty, unprincipled scheming). This fantasy land fascinated both Jacobean and Elizabethan England. It fed the popular prejudice that such foreign places were full of villainy, perversion and secret love affairs in which sexual passion broke all social rules. A number of plays are based on real-life scandals in Italy or Spain.

- Religious and moral hypocrisy
  The plays present both priests and 'religious' people as insincere and deceitful. Often virulently anti-Catholic (Jacobean England was a Protestant country), the plays strip away the outward appearance of religious honesty, revealing a diseased and dissolute reality beneath. Characters often speak of 'God' or 'sin' and show they are aware of the religious consequences of their evil actions – but they hypocritically carry on doing wrong!

- The '**malcontent**'
  This typical character of Jacobean tragedy is a troubled individual who comments caustically and critically on society and other characters. He is often the revengeful plotter, the agent of retribution. In John Marston's play *The Malcontent* (1603–1604), the malcontent's name is the key to his nature: Malvole = 'ill-wisher'. He displays his 'hydeous imagination' as he exposes the corruption of the court.

- Women
  Jacobean tragedy contains many notable portrayals of women. Although the women inhabit male-dominated worlds, many are confident and sensual, seeking to control their own lives. But most end as victims, blamed and distrusted by the male characters who hold them responsible for the corruption and ruin of powerful men.

- Language
  A sardonic, sombre tone characterises the intense, vibrant language of the plays. Vivid imagery expresses the plays' relish for corruption, sexual passion, disease, decay and death.

▶ Use the seven features above to invent a Jacobean tragedy. Write a single paragraph containing each of these features as a plot summary of your imaginary play. You could, for example, begin like this: 'Malevolo, Duke of Naples, is filled with anger because ...'.

▶ To gain a first impression of Jacobean tragedy, read the extract from *The Revenger's Tragedy* on page 94. How many of the seven features above can you identify in this short extract?

Shakespeare wrote many of his plays during the reign of James I, so he is also a Jacobean dramatist. But his two 'revenge plays', *Titus Andronicus* (written about 1590) and *Hamlet* (1601) were written during Elizabeth I's reign. His Jacobean plays are almost all very different in subject, tone and language from the plays of other Jacobean dramatists. Those dramatists were almost certainly influenced by *Hamlet*, which set a standard for later revenge tragedies.

This book discusses the five Jacobean tragedies most frequently performed in the past 100 years, and which still appear regularly in stage productions today: *The White Devil* and *The Duchess of Malfi* by John Webster; *The Revenger's Tragedy*, *The Changeling* and *Women Beware Women* by Thomas Middleton. The following very brief plot summaries of these plays (and John Ford's *'Tis Pity She's a Whore*, also frequently performed today) will give you a first flavour of Jacobean tragedy. Although John Ford wrote the play around 1630, several years after the death of James I, it is usually considered to be one of the greatest examples of Jacobean tragedy. *The Changeling* is set in Alicante, Spain. All the others are set in Italy.

The White Devil: Vittoria Corombona, the 'white devil', involves her brother Flamineo (a malcontent) in a series of murders to achieve her adulterous desires. She is accused of murder and adultery and sentenced to imprisonment as a whore, but is rescued by her lover, who is later murdered by a revenger, Francisco. Brother and sister fall out, she wishes to kill him, but both are killed by agents of Francisco.

The Duchess of Malfi: The Duchess, a widow, secretly marries her steward, Antonio. Her brothers, Duke Ferdinand and the Cardinal, employ Bosola, an ex-galley slave (and malcontent), to spy on her. He discovers her secret, and he and Ferdinand mentally torture her with madmen and the mock corpse of her husband. She and her children are strangled. Ferdinand goes mad, and thinks he is a wolf. In a final bloodbath, Bosola, now remorseful, seeks revenge. But he accidently kills Antonio, then slays the Cardinal, is himself killed by Ferdinand who is in turn killed by Antonio's friends.

The Revenger's Tragedy: Vindice (a malcontent), holding the skull of his beloved lady, swears revenge against the Duke who has poisoned her. He disguises himself, enters the service of the Duke's son and tricks the Duke into kissing the poisoned skull. The Duke's family all plot against each other, and the play ends with a masque at which all the Duke's sons and stepsons are killed. Vindice is sent for execution.

The Changeling: Beatrice Joanna hires the facially disfigured Deflores to murder the man her father has chosen for her to marry. Deflores (a malcontent) does the killing, cuts off the murdered man's finger, then blackmails Beatrice into sex with him. She deceives her new husband Alsemero by substituting her maid in the bridal bed. The murdered man's brother seeks revenge, the murder is exposed, Deflores kills Beatrice, then himself. In the sub-plot, a lover disguises himself as a madman in an attempt to seduce the young wife of the owner of a house of mad people.

Women Beware Women: The Duke of Florence seduces Bianca, the wife of a poor clerk, and she becomes his mistress at court. Hippolito (an incestuous malcontent) kills the clerk, and the play ends in a masque at which Bianca commits suicide and, in a wholesale revenge massacre, characters are killed off with poisoned arrows, incense, deadly trapdoors and gold.

'Tis Pity She's a Whore: Giovanni incestuously loves his sister, Annabella. She marries the nobleman Soranzo, whose violent and cunning servant Vasques (a malcontent) discovers that Giovanni is the father of Annabella's expected child. Soranzo plans vengeance, but Giovanni kills his sister, cuts out her heart, kills Soranzo, and is himself killed by Vasques.

▶ Remind yourself of the seven features of Jacobean tragedy listed on pages 10–11. Find how each (except language) is represented in the play summaries above.

The origins of tragedy

Tragedy had its origins in ancient Greece. At religious festivals, drama and poetry presented high status men and women suffering grief and calamity brought about by their own actions (or by the gods).

'Tragedy' comes from the Greek *tragoidia*, meaning 'goat play'. Quite what goats have to do with stories of the suffering and fall of great heroes is not clear. One possible explanation might be that of the 'scapegoat': somebody who takes the blame for others' misdeeds. For example, in biblical times a priest would symbolically load all the sins of the community on to a goat, and the animal was then driven out into the wilderness. The action was believed to remove the sins from that society. In tragedy, the hero might be seen as such a scapegoat: a sacrifice to remove sins and so appease the gods.

Aristotle on tragedy

As Shakespeare, Webster and Middleton wrote their plays, they had in mind certain traditions, conventions and styles of tragedy. They would have been familiar with the writings of the Greek philosopher **Aristotle** (384-322 BC), whose assumptions about the nature of tragedy can be briefly summarised:

- A tragedy portrays a serious, complete, and important action involving pain or destruction.

- A tragedy shows the fall of an important person from happiness and prosperity into misery and catastrophe (this unexpected reversal of fortune is called *peripeteia*).

- The suffering and fall results from one or more causes:
  – some fatal flaw or frailty of personality (for example, *hubris* = overweening pride)
  – some error of judgement (*hamartia*)

– something of which the character is ignorant.

- The hero moves from ignorance to knowledge, coming to recognise clearly what causes his suffering (*anagnorisis* = recognition).

- Tragedy arouses pity and fear in the spectator, and succeeds in purging and purifying such emotions (*catharsis*).

Assignments

1 Think about the Shakespearean or Jacobean tragedy you know best, and suggest whether and how it matches each element of Aristotle's definition. (If you are not, at this moment, familiar with a Shakespearean or Jacobean tragedy, think of any play, novel or film that you consider a 'tragedy'. Does it fulfil each element of Aristotle's definition?)

2 Why do audiences pay to watch tragedies: harrowing plays about suffering and death? Do they 'enjoy' tragedies even though they feel uncomfortable watching them? Begin by talking about your own responses to plays or films that you consider to be tragedies.

3 In 1615 John Greene wrote about the tragedies being performed on stage in his time:

The matter of tragedies is haughtiness, arrogancy, ambition, pride, injury, anger, wrath, envy, hatred, contention, war, murder, cruelty, rapine, incest, rovings, depredations, piracies, spoils, robberies, rebellions, treasons, killing, hewing, stabbing, dagger-drawing, fighting, butchery, treachery, villainy, …

Consider each word of Greene's description in turn and see if you can identify an example of it in one or other of the play summaries on pages 12–13. Then decide whether you think Greene is giving an accurate or a distorted view of Jacobean tragedy, and whether or not he approved of it.

4 Make your own checklist to help your memory! Quickly read again pages 7–13. Then close the book, write 'Shakespearean and Jacobean Tragedy' on a sheet of paper, and spend a few minutes jotting down whatever words come into your mind. Then use your words to construct an ordered list. Finally, open the book again and remind yourself of words or phrases which you wish to add to your list.

2 | Contexts

- What inspired Shakespeare and the Jacobean dramatists to write their plays?

- What literature and drama influenced Shakespeare and the Jacobean playwrights?

- What features of Elizabethan and Jacobean England helped produce the tragedies?

- Is the personal experience of the playwrights reflected in the tragedies?

'Nothing will come of nothing'

What inspired Shakespeare to write his plays? The film *Shakespeare in Love* (1999) portrays a popular belief about the source of Shakespeare's creativity. It shows him suffering from 'writer's block', unable to put pen to paper, with no idea of how to write his next play. But all is resolved when he meets a beautiful young girl. His love for her sparks an overwhelming flow of creative energy – and he writes *Romeo and Juliet*!

It is an attractive idea, delightfully presented, but the truth of the matter is far more complex. Shakespeare (like Webster, Middleton and other playwrights of his time) was influenced by many factors other than personal experience. In this section you will be invited to think about the contexts from which the tragedies emerged: the wide range of different influences on Shakespeare and on other dramatists as they wrote their plays.

Shakespeare's friend and fellow playwright Ben Jonson famously said that Shakespeare 'was not for an age but for all time'. Many people have interpreted 'not for an age' as meaning that Shakespeare was a unique genius. They claim that his plays flowed solely from his imagination, and that he was independent of, and unaffected by, the society in which he lived. That romantic notion of the artist as solitary genius came into full flower in the early 19th century and has appealed greatly to people ever since.

But it is much more realistic to acknowledge that every writer, however gifted, is affected by the world in which he or she lives. Drama is a social activity: a collaboration of writers, actors and audience. In every historical age, the theatre is part of a network of other institutions and practices which influence the subject matter and style of presentation of plays. These 'contexts' include family, politics, religion, the economy, all kinds of daily activities and beliefs.

Shakespeare gave King Lear the line 'Nothing will come of nothing'. That comment expresses the basic assumption of this book. Shakespeare was a genius, but he was not a solitary genius, absolutely independent of his society, creating his plays from 'nothing'. Rather, like his fellow dramatists, he was acutely aware of the society of his time. Its history, language, culture, beliefs and conflicts were the raw materials on which his imagination worked. Elizabethan and Jacobean England provided the stimulating environment which fostered the creativity of Shakespeare and other playwrights.

▶ An image from Shakespeare's Sonnet 111 suggests that everyone is affected by the world in which they live:

> And almost thence my nature is subdued
> To what it works in, like the dyer's hand.

Just as dyers find their hands stained by the dyes with which they work, so each person's nature is 'subdued' (overpowered, determined) by the society in which they live. Talk together about how far you think you are 'free' of society, and how far you are conditioned by it. You will probably find it helpful to begin with very practical examples: are you free to fall in love with whoever you like? are you free to believe any religion you choose?

▶ Why didn't Shakespeare write science fiction, or about Japanese samurai? Make a list of topics about which Shakespeare and Jacobean playwrights could not have written. Why not?

What were the influences that helped produce the tragedies written by Shakespeare and his Jacobean contemporaries? The question of how far their personal experience is reflected in the plays is virtually impossible to answer (but see page 107). What can be done is an exploration of the world of Shakespeare and his fellow playwrights to identify the cultural, social and historical contexts that resourced their imaginations and provided subjects and issues to turn into drama. What follows is an account of the major contexts of Shakespearean and Jacobean tragedy.

Dramatic and literary contexts

Seneca (4 BC–65 AD)

The classical dramatist who had the greatest impact on the development of tragedy in Shakespeare's time was Seneca, the Roman philosopher and poet. Seneca found the material for his tragic dramas in Greek mythology, but his reworking of those ancient tales was done in a startling manner which greatly appealed to Elizabethan and Jacobean playwrights and audiences. The following features of Senecan drama made their mark on Shakespeare's tragedies, and even more so on the Jacobean tragedies.

- Seneca revelled in gory and macabre descriptions, and in sensational and shocking displays of violence and horror that produced a corpse-strewn stage (a style of theatre that in late 19th-century France came to be called *grand guignol*).

- Ghosts, witches, magic and other supernatural features appear frequently in Seneca's plays, and characters descend into madness.

- Revenge is the dominant motive that drives characters and provides dramatic suspense. Vengeance and excessive behaviour go hand in hand.

- Language is exaggerated and **hyperbolic** (obviously extravagant and 'over-the-top') Characters speak long, rhetorical monologues.

- Seneca's plays have a five-part structure, approximately as follows:
  Act 1: a ghost appeals for vengeance
  Act 2: the revenger plans revenge
  Act 3: the confrontation of avenger and victim
  Act 4: vengeance is prevented
  Act 5: revenge is completed.

- Some of Seneca's plays contain a play within a play (a device used for example in *Hamlet*).

A collection of Seneca's tragedies was published in 1581 and the impact on English drama was profound. It gave rise to a torrent of five-act revenge plays which enjoyed huge popular success. Most of those early plays have vanished into oblivion, but Seneca's influence on two playwrights, Thomas Kyd and Christopher Marlowe, in turn provided a context which produced its fullest flowering in the tragedies of Shakespeare and the Jacobeans, Webster and Middleton.

▶ Think about the Shakespearean or Jacobean tragedy you know best and suggest whether and how it matches each element of Senecan tragedy listed above. (If you are not, at this moment, familiar with a Shakespearean tragedy, think of any play or novel that you consider a 'tragedy'. Which elements of Senecan tragedy does it display?)

▶ Read the extracts from *Titus Andronicus* and *The Revenger's Tragedy* on pages 74 and 94. In what ways do they display evidence of the influence of Seneca?

Thomas Kyd (1558–1594)

In the early 1590s, Thomas Kyd's *The Spanish Tragedy* was a theatrical sensation. It packed in audiences, and was the talk of the town. The play is a bloody but searching examination of the relationship of revenge and justice. The main character, Hieronimo, the Knight Marshal of Spain, is driven into madness by the murder of his son Horatio. Hieronimo cannot obtain justice from the gods or the king, and so determines to achieve personal revenge. He prepares a play in which he will wreak vengeance on his son's killers:

> Behoves thee then, Hieronomo, to be revenged.
> The plot is laid of dire revenge:
> On then, Hieronimo, pursue revenge,
> For nothing wants but acting of revenge.

The play is heavily influenced by Seneca: it contains a ghost, a play within a play, madness and bloodshed. There are all kinds of gruesome events: hangings, suicides, a near burning at the stake, multiple stabbings. Threatened with torture, Hieronimo bites out his tongue, then kills another enemy and himself. The language is Senecan: exaggerated, hyperbolic, rhetorical.

The Spanish Tragedy is fast-moving and skilfully plotted. It focuses relentlessly on the working out of revenge. Revenge appears as a character throughout the play, as a kind of **Chorus** (narrator who introduces or comments on the play) and director of the action. Almost everyone in the play seeks revenge, prompted by all kinds of different motives: honour, love, envy, anger and grief.

The word 'revenge' echoes throughout the play: it opens with a ghost calling for revenge on his killer, and various characters make similar demands. Bel-imperia, the main female character, says she cannot find love again 'Till I revenge the death of my beloved'; and her enemy Balthazar decides 'Yet must I take revenge or die myself'. Kyd's Elizabethan audiences relished discovering how inventively each revenge or treachery would be carried out.

The play's appeal as a bloodthirsty cliff-hanger made it hugely popular. Kyd uses black humour and dramatic irony to increase audience enjoyment. In one scene, the murderer Pedringano is confident that he will be pardoned moments before the hangman can execute him. But the audience knows that the box which Pedringano thinks contains his pardon is empty. The condemned villain's confidence and mockery is fatally misplaced.

The Spanish Tragedy demonstrated how much audiences enjoyed plays in which murder breeds murder and almost every character intends harm to others. The astonishing success of Kyd's play undoubtedly influenced Shakespeare and the Jacobean dramatists. They took over many of the elements of Kyd's tragic model, but in their different ways transformed them, writing plays which have stood the test of time far more successfully than Kyd's. His bloodcurdler has virtually vanished from the theatre, but its influence cannot be underestimated.

Shakespeare's *Hamlet* owes it a debt, as does every Jacobean tragedy discussed in this book. A reminder of the key features of *The Spanish Tragedy* can help your understanding of its influence on Shakespearean and Jacobean tragedy:

- the close linking of justice and revenge
- the presentation of revenge as a sacred duty, where an individual, denied justice, takes the law into his or her own hands
- the portrayal of a hesitant revenger (foreshadowing Hamlet)
- madness
- extremes of emotion
- deceit and intrigue
- the supernatural.

▶ To gain an impression of Kyd's influence, use the summary above and suggest how each feature is represented in one Shakespearean and one Jacobean tragedy.

Christopher Marlowe (1564–1593)

Thomas Kyd was a successful and influential dramatist, but even his *Spanish Tragedy* was far outstripped in popularity and influence by the plays of Christopher Marlowe. The son of a Canterbury shoemaker, Marlowe was born in the same year as Shakespeare, achieved fame before him, but died young, killed in a tavern quarrel, aged only 29. His short life was turbulent, his reputation notorious. He was believed to be involved in spying activities, and was viewed as a dangerous subversive, accused of violence, atheism, blasphemy and homosexuality.

In spite of all the criticisms of his outrageous beliefs and private life, Marlowe's career as a playwright was meteoric. He shot to fame with a succession of plays that exposed the hypocrisy of religion and politics. His dramas portrayed heroic 'overreachers': men determined to impose their will on the world, to become the masters of their own fates. These aspiring hero-villains are corrupted and destroyed by their own soaring ambition and passions, and their rejection of conventional religion and morality.

Marlowe's first play *Tamburlaine the Great*, was staged when he was only 23. It shows Tamburlaine, a cruel and ferocious Scythian shepherd, becoming a world conqueror. The play was so successful that Marlowe followed it with an equally acclaimed sequel which further demonstrated his mastery of lyrical **blank verse**. The style, full of energy, resonance and pace, has become known as 'Marlowe's mighty line'. It can be seen to full effect in the scene where exhausted captive kings, lashed by Tamburlaine, draw his chariot on stage. Tamburlaine cries, as he whips them:

Holla, ye pamper'd jades of Asia!
What, can ye draw but twenty miles a day,
And have so proud a chariot at your heels,
And such a coachman as great Tamburlaine?

The Jew of Malta, described in its title as a tragedy, is grotesquely comic in many of its scenes. It portrays Barabas, a rich Jew whose wealth is wrongly seized by the Governor of Malta. In revenge, Barabas feels no pangs of conscience as he commits a series of terrible crimes. He kills his own daughter and an entire convent of nuns with poisoned porridge, and betrays Malta to the Turkish invaders. He finally falls victim to his own devices, falling into a cauldron he has prepared for his enemies at a banquet. At a time when church attendance was compulsory, Marlowe's critics would be horrified to hear his character Machiavel declare in the play's prologue:

I count religion but a childish toy,
And hold there is no sin but ignorance

Marlowe's plays move far beyond Senecan tragedy. His major characters have an inner life, a complex psychology of contradictory emotions and motives. This is most clearly seen in *The Tragical History of the Life and Death of Dr Faustus*. The play shows Faustus striking a pact to sell his soul to the Devil. The bargain is that the Devil will give Faustus 24 years in which he can do anything he pleases, aided by Mephostophilis, agent of the Devil. After that period, Faustus will be taken, body and soul, into hell. Faustus enjoys his years of licence, but at the end is pulled down into hell.

▶ Read Faustus' anguished final speech on pages 72–73. It is agreed by scholars to be one of the finest pieces of dramatic writing in English. Suggest some reasons why it is given such high status as poetic drama.

▶ Step into role as the young Shakespeare, Webster or Middleton. You want to make your career as a playwright, but have not yet begun. What can you learn from Marlowe's final lines for Faustus that will help your own writing of tragedy?

Folk tales and morality plays

The roots of Shakespearean and Jacobean tragedy reach back to folklore and to medieval church practices and teaching. Many folk tales (popular stories handed down by oral tradition) told of the fall of mighty rulers, and how the turning wheel of fortune affected kings and beggars alike. Such stories echoed the church's teaching, which insisted on the brevity of human glory, the fickleness of fate and the power of divine providence: God's intentions for humankind.

In medieval times, religious rituals gradually extended their scope, moving outside the church walls to open-air performances of Bible stories. For several hundred years, various groups such as town guilds or strolling players presented pageants and plays. These dramas used tales from the Christian tradition to reinforce the church's teaching on religion and morality. The style of such performances was bold, clear and spectacular. When Shakespeare wrote lines for Hamlet, complaining of bad actors ranting, he may be recalling such a pageant play about King Herod that he saw as a child:

> O it offends me to the soul to hear a robustious peri-wig pated fellow tear a passion to totters, to very rags ... I would have such a fellow whipped for o'erdoing Termagant – it out-Herods Herod.

To hold their audiences, these local adaptations included a good deal of villainy and suspense. 'Morality plays' became extremely popular. These plays dealt with the problems and dilemmas which afflict human beings, and portrayed them as battles between good and evil for the soul of Everyman or Mankind. Characters in morality plays were personified human vices or virtues: Greed, Lust, Envy, Mercy or Justice, etc. These stock types, or stereotypes, represented forces that could save or damn every living person, gaining them a place in heaven or condemning them to everlasting suffering in hell.

Folk tales and morality plays helped to prepare the ground for Shakespearean and Jacobean tragedy in their stock situations (humans caught up in terrible dilemmas), their themes (notably the struggle of good and evil), and their characters. Probably the most enjoyed character was Vice, a boastful trickster, a mischievous figure full of manic energy who tempted young men away from virtue. Vice was undoubtedly meant to portray evil, he was an enemy of mankind, an agent of the Devil. But his humour and trickery endeared him to audiences, whom he would confide in either by direct address, or in 'asides'. Vice is easily recognised as an ancestor of Shakespeare's villains, Richard III, Iago and Edmund, and of the 'malcontents' and revengers who appear in Jacobean tragedies (see page 25).

▶ For hundreds of years before Shakespeare wrote his play *Romeo and Juliet*, folk tales existed about young lovers who perished because of their families' hatred for each other. Turn back to the brief play summaries on pages 9–10 and 12–13. Suggest which tragedies seem to you to have the qualities of a folk tale. Why?

Literary sources

Literature provides the clearest evidence that Shakespeare was strongly influenced by the culture within which he lived. For each of his tragedies, it is possible to identify what he had read which gave him ideas for the story, characters and particular scenes. He used his imagination to mould what he read into dramatic form.

For example, it is obvious that Shakespeare had a copy of Sir Thomas North's translation of Plutarch's *The Lives of the Noble Grecians and Romans* (published in English in 1579) on his table as he wrote *Julius Caesar, Antony and Cleopatra*, and *Coriolanus*. Although he adds characters and makes all kinds of revisions, omitting or inventing episodes for dramatic effect, Shakespeare often follows Plutarch's story very closely. Some passages are directly based on North's language, but comparison reveals how his changes increase theatrical and poetic effect. The most famous example is the description of Cleopatra in Act 2 Scene 2: lines 201–228. Here are just a few lines. What changes did Shakespeare make, and why?

> ... to take her barge in the river of Cydnus, the poop whereof was of gold, the sails of purple, and the oars of silver, which kept stroke in rowing after the sound of the music of flutes, hautboys, citherns, viols
>
> (Plutarch)

> The barge she sat in, like a burnished throne
> Burned on the water. The poop was beaten gold;
> Purple the sails, and so perfumed
> That the winds were lovesick with them. The oars were silver,
> Which to the tune of flutes kept stroke, and made
> The water which they beat to follow faster,
> As amorous of their strokes.
>
> (Shakespeare)

For *Romeo and Juliet*, Shakespeare's major source was a long poem by Arthur Brooke, 'The Tragical History of Romeus and Juliet', written in 1562. For *Othello*, Shakespeare found his plot in a collection of Italian narratives, *Hecatommithi* by Giraldo Cinthio (which he might have read in Italian or French). For *Macbeth*, he used Raphael Holinshed's *Chronicles of England, Scotland and Ireland*, first published in 1577. Shakespeare invented the character of Lady Macbeth from a few lines he read in the Chronicles that Macbeth's wife wished to be queen and was very ambitious. His portrayal of Richard III derives from Sir Thomas More's highly biased *History of Richard III*, which was re-used in Holinshed's *Chronicles*.

Hamlet seems to be based on a 12th-century revenge story about an early Prince of Denmark, Amleth. The story appears in a 16th-century book by Saxo Grammaticus: *Historiae Danicae*. The old story has recognisable similarities with *Hamlet*. Amleth's father defeats the King of Norway, but is murdered by his own brother who marries the queen, Amleth's mother. In pursuit of revenge, Amleth feigns madness. But Shakespeare significantly changes the fate of the character who overhears Amleth's private conversation with his mother. In the play, Hamlet thrusts his sword through an arras (curtain), and kills Polonius. In the story,

Amleth pretends to be a cockerel, finds the spy under a straw mattress, kills him, chops him up, cooks him and feeds him to the pigs!

Other literary sources of the Jacobean tragedies considered in this book include letters or documents which reported scandals in Italy or Spain. These are often little known, but a book which certainly influenced Shakespeare and the Jacobean playwrights was Niccolo Machiavelli's *The Prince* (1532). Even to those who had not read the book, its purpose and argument were well known. *The Prince* was a handbook for rulers about the use of deceit in statecraft. Machiavelli urged rulers to use any means, however unethical or immoral, to stay in power. His instruction in practical politics was a set of ruthless and manipulative prescriptions to ensure no-one could succeed in overthrowing a monarch. Machiavelli had a low and cynical opinion of human nature:

> For one can say this generally of men: that they are ungrateful, fickle, pretenders and dissemblers, evaders of danger, eager for gain. While you do them good, they are yours.

In the drama of Elizabethan and Jacobean England, the *machiavel* (a villainous plotter and schemer) became a familiar figure who delighted in wrongdoing and used poison, sword or torture to achieve his ends. In Christopher Marlowe's *The Jew of Malta*, Machiavel introduces the play and tells how scheming manipulators who follow his advice ('my climbing followers') may rise to the top. Such portrayals of scheming and unscrupulous foreigners greatly appealed to the English audiences of the time, and the popular conception of Machiavelli had a great influence on Webster and Middleton.

▶ Research the tragedy you are studying to identify the literary source (stories or plays) used as inspiration for the plot, or for particular episodes or passages (pages 55 and 58 can help you). Try to find a copy of the source material (this is much easier for Shakespeare's tragedies than for Jacobean tragedies), and examine how it was turned it into drama by Shakespeare or other playwrights.

The condition of England

The world Shakespeare and his fellow dramatists knew was quite unlike the myth of 'Merrie England' ruled over by 'Good Queen Bess'. This false stereotype portrayed happy peasants frolicking around maypoles in a society where everyone knew and was content with their allotted position in life. The reality was quite different. In Shakespeare's England, great prosperity and great poverty lived cheek by jowl. England was growing richer, but the new wealth was unequally distributed, and the imbalance created dangerous unrest.

Manufacturing and commerce increased England's prosperity. So too did the geographical discoveries which opened up new worlds, and by colonisation and conquest added to England's wealth. A flourishing import and export trade developed. Wine and rich cloth flowed in and textiles from England's flourishing wool industry flowed out. The tragedies are full of references to such trade. In *Richard III*, Clarence is drowned in a butt of malmsey (sweet wine). In *King Lear*, Kent rages at Oswald as a 'three-suited, hundred pound, filthy worsted-stocking knave', and Lear comments bitterly on the expensive gorgeous clothes his daughter Regan wears 'Which scarcely keeps thee warm'.

There was a huge gap between rich and poor. A small minority was very rich, but for most English men and women life consisted of unremitting labour, poverty and struggle. Many poor men and women were driven into beggary or crime. England was a discontented country in which social abuses aggravated the plight of the poor.

Inflation, increased taxation, threats of war, unemployment and low wages made worse the condition of the labouring class. Their misery was increased by enclosures of common land on which they relied to help them survive. Enclosures helped a minority to grow even richer at the expense of the great majority. Natural disasters of successive harvest failures added to the misery and near starvation, and led to food shortages. There were violent riots against enclosures. At the start of *Coriolanus*, Shakespeare may be using his knowledge of such protests: the play begins with the plebeians in revolt against the patricians' hoarding of corn. In *Julius Caesar* he showed just what the authorities feared: an out-of-control mob burning and rampaging, and killing Cinna the Poet for no other reason than his name.

▶ To experience the contrast between the ideal and the actual condition of England, read the extract from *Richard II* on pages 77–78. How far do you think Shakespeare is criticising the England of his times in this extract?

Social hierarchy – and the malcontent

Elizabethan and Jacobean England was sharply hierarchical, like a very tall pyramid. At the top of the pyramid was the monarch, then the aristocrats, then the knights and gentry, then the citizens or burgesses, the yeomen. At the bottom was the great majority of the population, with no power, no voice, no wealth or possessions: a huge mass whose function was to labour and to be ruled.

There were no political parties similar to those today. Instead, there were groups and factions, held together by religious beliefs and common interests of wealth and power. During the reign of James I, the power of the monarch and the old aristocracy was increasingly challenged by the gentry and the merchants who were angered more and more by the extravagance of James and his court. A further threat lay in the protests of the ordinary people against their poverty. Each faction viewed the other with distrust or hostility.

In this atmosphere of suspicion and fear, with no television or newspapers, news passed mainly by word of mouth. Gossip and rumours flourished. Long after the defeat of the Armada in 1588, there were constant alarms about a possible Spanish invasion. The monarchy was a great source of wild speculation. Many false stories about Queen Elizabeth's ill-health spread like wildfire. In 1606 a rumour ran that King James had been assassinated at Woking. There were all kinds of tales about the many riots, brawls and disorders that occurred in London and around the country. In *Hamlet* the people who spread such rumours are dismissed as 'buzzers' who 'infect' the listeners' ears.

In such a climate, it was not surprising that the Government wished to control news and debate. Free discussion was distrusted by those in power. It was seen as a potent source of treason. To detect and defeat subversion the state maintained an extensive network of spies and informers. Polonius in *Hamlet* is often thought of as Shakespeare's portrait of Lord Burghley, Elizabeth's chief minister, who believed that close surveillance of suspected dissidents was necessary to maintain order. Polonius secretly spies on Hamlet, using his own daughter Ophelia as bait.

Shakespearean and Jacobean tragedies invited audiences to witness the fall of great people. Such displays of the decline of the rich and powerful were both fascinating and threatening. The authorities valued order, but what they called 'order' was a justification of inequality. The rich and powerful often spoke of 'the commonwealth', but their conception of such a society did not include any real change in the hierarchy. Everyone had a place and was expected to know it and keep it.

But such thinking did not rule out social mobility, and many individuals seized opportunities to acquire wealth and rise up the social scale. There were plenty of examples of social climbing, not least Shakespeare himself who ended his life as a rich, land-owning citizen of Stratford. The determination and ability to rise in society is expressed by Marlowe's Tamburlaine as he throws off his shepherd's clothes: 'Lie here, ye weeds that I disdain to wear', and by Edmund in *King Lear* who declares he will use any trick to help him gain wealth and claw his way upwards:

> Let me, if not by birth, have lands by wit.
> All with me's meet that I can fashion fit.

Edmund is an example of the 'malcontent', a familiar figure of the times, both in real life and in the theatre. The malcontent is a character type in Elizabethan and Jacobean drama. He is like 'the angry young man' of the 1960s: a discontented or melancholy man, who rails bitterly at the society in which he lives. The malcontent was based on a fashionable pose that many courtiers adopted in Shakespeare's time. Such a man would express dissatisfaction with himself and with everything around him: family, state, nature itself. Unhappy, and critical of everything and everybody, the malcontent was socially and psychologically dislocated. But he was also often an opportunist, seeking his own personal advancement in the society against which he raged so caustically.

Different kinds of malcontent appear in plays of the time. There is no single type; they appear in all kinds of guises. One of the best known appears in a comedy: the bitter but comic Jaques in *As You Like It*. A much fiercer critic of humanity is Thersites in *Troilus and Cressida*. In the tragedies, characters playing the malcontent role include such diverse individuals as:

* the evil villains Iago in *Othello*, Edmund in *King Lear*, Aaron in *Titus Andronicus*
* the deeply introspective Prince Hamlet, unhappy, dispossessed of his right to succeed his father
* the blunt soldier Enobarbus, critical of Antony's folly, and finally disgusted with himself
* the cynical Cassius in *Julius Caesar*
* the misanthropic (humankind-hating) Timon of Athens
* the 'outsiders' of Jacobean revenge tragedies who, though of low social status, play a major part in the working out of vengeance: Vindice, Hippolito, Bosola, Flamineo, Deflores. All are agents and victims of revenge plots.

▶ To see the most extreme portrayal of a malcontent, read the extract from *Timon of Athens* on page 89. Make a list of all he condemns or curses in Athens, and suggest whether you think any might be Shakespeare's veiled criticism of his own society.

Death, disease and violence

The audiences of the time were well prepared to watch and respond to the shocking events and themes of tragedy. The subject matter reflected familiar aspects of their everyday world. It was what life was like.

There was a preoccupation with death and decay. Death's heads and other reminders of death (*memento mori*) were kept by individuals, or given as gifts as a reminder of human mortality. Disease and death were ever-present for most families in Elizabethan and Jacobean England. Average life expectancy was little more than 30 years, and there was a high rate of infant mortality. In some districts only 50% of children survived to their 15th birthday. Sexual diseases ('the pox') were common.

The plague was a regular visitor to city and country alike, and frequently caused the closure of the theatres. In London in 1603 over one sixth of the population died in an outbreak of the plague. Few anaesthetics were available. For most people, medical treatment was rudimentary, more a matter of ignorance and superstition than true knowledge of what caused the disease. It was hardly surprising that cures were only infrequently achieved. The many images of disease in *Hamlet* and in Webster's plays convey the theme of corruption, but they also reflect the familiar experience of the audience.

Shakespeare's contemporaries were accustomed to macabre and violent spectacles which appealed to some of the same instincts that responded to tragedy. Elizabethans and Jacobeans lived in a hard, violent world, and were neither squeamish nor politically correct. They visited asylums to laugh at madmen (just as happens in *The Changeling*). The cruel 'sports' of cockfighting, bull-baiting and bear-baiting attracted large audiences. When Macbeth, surrounded by his enemies, declares 'They have tied me to a stake; I cannot fly,/ But bear-like I must fight the course', spectators at the Globe would recall the bear-baiting pit only a few yards distant.

Violence and crime were everyday facts of life, from assault and murder to horse stealing, burglary and highway robbery. The Jacobean revenge tragedies appealed to audiences all too aware of the revenge impulse that often sprang from the violence of everyday life. But violence had other consequences. Punishment was visibly on display. There were many examples of public shamings in which offenders sat in the stocks, were tied to whipping posts, endured the pain of branding, or having ears or hands cut off. Witches and heretics were executed, often burned alive.

Public executions, watched by thousands, contained the cruellest tortures, as the condemned man was hanged, drawn and quartered (hung, but cut down before death, disembowelled, and chopped into pieces). The tragedies contain reminders of the everyday experience of crime and punishment. *The Spanish Tragedy* reflects the vogue for executions as dramatic entertainments. At the end of *Macbeth*, the sight of Macbeth's severed head was a dramatic reminder of the sinister display on London Bridge of the heads of executed traitors.

▶ Consider the tragedy you are studying and list the instances of violence and brutality it contains. Imagine you are directing the play. Prepare a talk that you will give to the actors before you begin rehearsing. Your talk explains your views on how the violence will be presented on stage and the effect you hope those stagings will have on the audience.

The subordination of women

Men were firmly in control in Elizabethan and Jacobean England. Women's status and roles were subject to the tyranny of patriarchy (rule by men). The husband and father ruled the family, just as a lord dominated his household, a monarch reigned over the state, and God held sway over all. Women had limited personal autonomy, far less than men. Their rights were restricted, legally, socially and economically.

Although England had a woman as its monarch for 40 years, and although Queen Elizabeth I did enjoy real power, her case was highly unusual. England was in effect a world ruled by males. The accession of King James did little or nothing to improve women's lot. His personal dislike of women was well known. The expectations for most women in England was that they should obey men, stay at home and raise a family. They should keep silent and get on with the housekeeping. Their valued virtues were chastity, modesty, obedience and faithfulness to their husbands.

Women who spoke up, who wanted 'liberty', were regarded with suspicion, and risked being labelled as a 'scold' or a 'shrew'. Articulate or angry women were seen as a threat to civil order. Harsh punishments were imposed on them: the ducking stool (being tied to a chair and ducked in a river), the bridle (a metal bit across the mouth), slapping, 'carting' (being carried around the town or village in mockery) and being made scapegoats for local ills. Old, ugly or eccentric women risked being demonised and accused of witchcraft.

There was a widely established prejudice that women were a different species from men, far inferior to them in rational thought, and led solely by their emotions. The pernicious views of John Knox, a Scottish Protestant preacher, expressed in his 'First Blast of the Trumpet against the Monstrous Regiment of Women' (1558), were enthusiastically believed. Knox claimed that nature creates women as

> weak, frail, impatient, feeble and foolish: and experience hath declared them to be unconstant, variable, cruel, and lacking the spirit of counsel and regiment. ('regiment' = order, self-control)

Compared with males, women received little education. They had no political voice or power. Forbidden from holding political or church office, the only career open to them was that of wife and mother. Single women enjoyed some freedom. They could sign contracts and inherit land and own property. But as soon as they married, those limited freedoms disappeared. Their property became their husband's and they became subject to their husband's rule across all areas of life.

Women were regarded as possessions, as capital to be exploited in profitable marriage matches. They were virtually helpless pawns in the power games of their male relatives because men had the major say over who the females in the family married. In the five Jacobean revenge tragedies discussed in this book, each main female character is treated by men as a chattel (a possession), to be disposed of as men wish.

But in spite of all the restrictions, it is clear that women possessed some measure of freedom. They ran the household affairs, took part in all kinds of entertainment, and sometimes played key roles in managing business affairs. Although men ruled, women's influence was obvious in many spheres of life, and their status and actions were hotly debated.

Visitors to England often commented on the greater freedom English women enjoyed in comparison with other European females. English women frequently attended theatre performances, where they saw portrayals of females on stage (albeit acted by males) which challenged the idea that women were subordinate. Drama presented many confident, quick-witted women who challenged male authority and who sought to take control over their own lives. A remarkable number of articulate and intelligent women feature in the tragedies: Cleopatra, Juliet, Lady Macbeth, Cordelia, Gonerill and Regan, Volumnia, Vittoria Corombona, Beatrice-Joanna, Bianca. They play a commanding part in the action, and in different ways endeavour to take charge of their own lives. Webster's *The Duchess of Malfi* shows the plight of such a woman trapped and finally killed by the patriarchal authority of family and state.

▶ Read two of the following extracts and suggest how you think contemporary audiences responded to the women in these episodes: *Romeo and Juliet* (page 78), *King Lear* (page 83), *The Duchess of Malfi* (page 92) and *The White Devil* (page 90). What is your own response to the way the extracts portray women?

The Jacobean court

The English court was the seat of state power, and was fiercely elitist and exclusive. A small number of aristocrats dominated court life, determined to increase their own influence and to keep outsiders from gaining similar power. The atmosphere was one of ambition and intrigue, with courtiers scheming to improve their social position and wealth. Queen Elizabeth had kept some measure of financial and moral control over the worst extravagances of her nobles, but even in her time the reputation of the court for rottenness was widespread. In 1592 Thomas Nashe in *Pierce Pennilesse: his supplication to the Devil*, said that a courtier's companions were 'Pride, Riot and Whoredom'.

Under King James, graft and corruption became all-pervasive. It was a well-known scandal that King James sold titles shamelessly. In the first year of his reign, James created 838 new knights, each of whom paid the king for the privilege. Every office was available at a price. Some critics have interpreted Malcolm's promotion of his thanes and kinsmen at the end of *Macbeth* ('Henceforth be earls') as Shakespeare's veiled criticism of King James' practice.

Vain and ambitious courtiers went into debt in their pursuit of prestige and 'nobility'. The court was a happy hunting ground for profiteers and adventurers, who plotted and flattered for social and financial gain. Distrust and suspicion was widespread as courtiers competed with each other for King James' favour. James himself spent lavishly and seemed little concerned about his courtiers' obvious corruption and extravagant lifestyles.

Sexual corruption flourished alongside financial corruption. The court was renowned as a place of sexual freedom, of pimps and procuresses, and kept women. The corruption and lust of Italian or Spanish courts depicted by Webster and the other Jacobean dramatists echoed the realities of the court of King James where machiavellianism (scheming) and sycophancy (servile and fawning flattery) were common practices.

The court was the centre of aristocratic display and conspicuous consumption. Machiavelli had claimed that political power was maintained through display and spectacle. The courts of Elizabeth and James confirmed that claim. Music, dancing, plays and masques (spectacular and costly entertainments) had been a prime feature of Elizabeth's court and became even more popular in James'. The appeal of such displays is reflected in contemporary plays. A 'play within a play' bloodily ends *The Spanish Tragedy*; *Hamlet* also contains a play within a play and a Dumbshow (which is a kind of masque); the masque in *The Revenger's Tragedy* begins with the chilling stage direction 'Enter the Masque of Revengers', which is the prelude to multiple killings.

Courtiers revelled in luxury, flaunting their wealth in extravagant, costly dress. In an attempt to protect social order, sumptuary laws (regulating expensive clothing) decreed that people should dress according to their social status, and tried to restrict wearing of certain fabrics to the aristocracy. The tragedies criticise such extravagance, showing that outward appearance does not match inner reality. Hamlet knows he has 'that within which passes show', and dismisses clothes as 'trappings'. King Lear identifies how fine dress covers corruption:

> Robes and furred gowns hide all. Plate sin with gold,
> And the strong lance of justice hurtless breaks;
> Arm it in rags, a pygmy's straw does pierce it

Under Elizabeth many of the nobility had taken every opportunity to increase their wealth. The extract from *Richard II* on page 77 describes England as 'leased out' and bound 'with inky blots and rotten parchment bonds'. Noblemen exploited the country through monopolies, enclosing land, and all kinds of commercial ventures. Monopolies were granted on many products, for example on window glass, starch, vinegar, playing cards and mathematical instruments. Personal monopolies were revoked under King James, but many nobles retained control, and further increased their wealth. Courtiers with monopolies did not like their exploitation to be exposed, and pressure was brought to bear on critics of the practice. In the Quarto version of *King Lear* (1608), the Fool comments on how 'lords and great men' want a part of any monopoly (Act 1 Scene 4). The remark was cut from the Folio version of the play (1623), possibly because of some kind of censorship. (A Quarto is about the size of this book. A Folio is four times larger.)

King James believed in 'the divine right of kings', the doctrine that the monarch is God's deputy on earth. James therefore claimed that to disobey or defy his wishes was to disobey God: opposition to the king was the same as blasphemy and should be similarly harshly punished. But James was all too aware of his own mortality and that challenges to his rule always threatened. When he appeared in public he wore thickly padded body armour beneath his gorgeous costumes to guard against the assassin's knife. The various dukes portrayed in the Jacobean revenge tragedies share James' stiff-necked, unyielding certainty about his own superiority, and their bloody endings may be a veiled reminder of the fate that awaits such rigid autocrats.

▶ Choose one Jacobean and one Shakespearean tragedy that contains a court. Make a list of the ways in which each contains some of the above features of the English court. What do you think is the attitude of Shakespeare, Webster or Middleton to those features, and to the court of King James?

Religion

In Shakespeare's England, religion and the state were inextricably intertwined. Throughout the 16th century the country swung between Catholicism and Protestantism. In 1533–1534, England became a Protestant country when King Henry VIII broke religious links with Rome. Catholicism and the Pope were replaced by Protestantism with the king at its head. From Henry's time on, the monarch became the 'supreme head of the church in England'. Under Henry's daughter Mary, England officially reverted to Catholicism, but returned to Protestantism under Elizabeth and her successors.

Protestants were hounded and burnt in Queen Mary's reign; under Elizabeth, it was the turn of Catholics to be persecuted and executed. Each faction believed that God was on its side, but under Mary, religious allegiance was to Roman Catholicism and the Pope in Rome, under Elizabeth and James to Protestantism and the English crown. The result was that Elizabethan and Jacobean England was a country where Catholics were distrusted and feared. In Protestant minds, Catholics were seen as superstitious and corrupt, obsessed with rituals and idols, always seeking political influence, worldly power and riches.

Throughout Elizabeth's reign, England was at war with different Catholic states. The defeat of the Spanish armada in 1588 was an occasion of great rejoicing.

Catholics were frequently suspected of conspiracies against Queen Elizabeth. The threat was very real because the Pope declared Elizabeth to be a heretic, and promised salvation in heaven to any Catholic who assassinated her. Later, a group of Catholic plotters organised the Gunpowder Plot of 1605, an unsuccessful attempt to blow up King James and parliament.

The most extreme critics of Catholicism were the Puritans. 'Puritan' was originally used as term of abuse in the 1560s. But by the time Shakespeare began writing his plays, it had been enthusiastically adopted by those Protestants who considered themselves purer, more perfect and more godly than their fellow Christians.

Puritans saw themselves as the only true believers. They detested all the show, spectacle and ceremony associated with Catholicism, preferring simplicity in worship and dress. They therefore wanted the reform of the church which had begun under Henry VIII to go much further, getting rid of bishops, simplifying church rituals, dress and worship.

The Puritans were not only virulently anti-Catholic. They were extreme in their stinging criticism of swearing, drunkenness and fornication. They condemned maypole dancing, gambling and other popular pursuits. Austere and joyless, the Puritans were vehemently critical of the stage, denouncing plays and players as immoral and blasphemous. They condemned the cross-dressing boys who played women's roles, claiming the practice provoked illicit sexual desires in audiences.

Whereas the Puritans saw religion pervading all aspects of life, the state used it directly as an instrument of control. Everyone was required by law to attend Sunday worship in church. Those who refused to attend ('recusants') were fined heavily. The law also demanded that in church the homilies were read aloud each Sunday. These were a set of instructions requiring unquestioning obedience to the monarch and to those in power. Church-going was thus an unqualified confirmation of state as well as divine power. Its preaching was intended to outlaw protest or dissent.

But even without such compulsion, and irrespective of whether a person was Protestant or Catholic, virtually everybody cared passionately about religious belief. Religion was ever present, a source of both comfort and anxiety. People worried about the state of their souls, about sin, and about what would happen after death. The question of salvation obsessed them: would they go to heaven or hell? Would they, like Hamlet's father's ghost, have to spend time in purgatory, a place of terrible suffering where sins were burnt and purged away? Their anxiety was increased by the loss of certainty that religion once afforded.

The break with Rome had shattered the old certainties of religion. Shakespeare and the Jacobean playwrights knew the Bible well and assumed that whoever watched their plays would possess similar knowledge. But there were now different versions of Christianity to believe, and Protestantism shifted responsibility for choice on to the individual. Characters in the tragedies frequently display the worried conscience that resulted from the lack of certainty and from individual choice.

The view that religion held all the answers to human questions was further undermined by advances in science. Francis Bacon (1561–1626) argued that scientific method (careful observation of physical events, reason and induction), was the route to knowledge. Such empiricism (scientific method) very obviously left out God as the source of knowledge. Established beliefs were challenged by scientific discoveries. To give only one example, Copernicus demonstrated that the sun, not the earth, was the centre of the universe. This 'de-centring' raised troubling questions about humanity itself: could religion still provide answers to the purpose of life itself?

For Protestants, death was especially terrifying. Protestantism taught the value of the individual conscience, and so heightened the sense of individual uniqueness. For many Protestants, this awareness of personal identity made death a tragedy of extinction, because it destroyed all those qualities that made up and were valued by individuals: the inward qualities of love, self, imagination. Hamlet's soliloquy 'To be or not to be?' expresses the fears of those Protestants who had rejected the old certainties, but were still unsure of what will happen after death.

Such forebodings are reflected in all the tragedies. Each is characterised by religious anxiety. Even those tragedies which do not have a Christian setting (for example, the Roman tragedies) show concern for the afterlife, for dying well, for 'the gods'. *King Lear* has a pre-Christian setting, and characters appeal to classical gods, but it bears evidence of troubled religious preoccupations. The gods are seen as malicious:

As flies to wanton boys are we to the gods,
They kill us for their sport.

Even in Christian settings, as in *The Duchess of Malfi*, God can seem indifferent to human fate:

We are merely the stars' tennis-balls, struck and bandied
Which way please them

▶ Read Hamlet's soliloquy on page 80. Then step into role as a director who wishes to put on a production of *Hamlet* to bring out the religious significance of the play. Write detailed notes on how you would stage the soliloquy.

Contempt for foreigners

It was a time of exploration and conquest. The feats of English sailors and improvements in navigation expanded England's empire through conquest and colonisation, particularly in the New World of America and the Caribbean. The greater confidence which came from expansion abroad and at home fostered a growing sense of national identity. But as the English felt more secure in themselves as a nation, they developed unflattering or contemptuous views of foreigners.

The tragedies are full of casual and intended negative portrayals of aliens, reflecting popular attitudes of the time. When Shakespeare used Jews, Turks, Indians or Africans in his language of abuse and insult, he was doing little more than expressing common language use and beliefs. Jacobean revenge tragedies similarly mirrored and fed popular prejudices as they exposed Italians and Spaniards to scorn and ridicule, depicting foreign courts as full of murder, lust and vice.

Italy and Spain were seen as corrupt countries, where treachery and perversion flourished. Italians and Spaniards were regarded by many English men and women as deceitful, unreliable and vengeful, always working out treacherous plots and intrigues. Some of the roots of that suspicion lay in religion: the anti-Catholicism fostered by King Henry VIII's break with Rome.

▶ Consider one tragedy by Shakespeare and one by Webster or Middleton. Identify the attitude towards foreigners (non-English) that you think each play expresses. If you were directing one of the tragedies, are there passages you would cut in performance? (For example, some productions cut the witches' references to Jew, Turk and Tartar in the cauldron scene in *Macbeth*.)

London and the theatre

The experience of living in London was a rich influence on the tragedies of Shakespeare and his fellow playwrights. It provided them with audiences, money and a fruitful resource for their imaginations. London was the most important city in England, both the capital and a thriving port. It housed the royal court, parliament, the city guilds and companies, the law courts. It was the centre of political, commercial, legal and intellectual life, and was home to a flourishing publishing industry.

As the financial centre of England, London was where money was raised for commerce and industry, legitimate trading ventures and piracy. Huge volumes of exports and imports went through London's docks. The city bustled with politicians, aristocrats, soldiers and sailors, lawyers, poets and churchmen, foreign visitors, merchants and traders, all kinds of workers and apprentices – and a teeming underclass of prostitutes, beggars, thieves and villains.

Brothels and taverns enjoyed lively trade within sight of churches and the homes of respectable citizens. London's open drains ensured an almost perpetual stink. The reminders of violence, personal and state, were daily sights. In 1598 freshly painted whipping posts were set up all over the city.

Londoners were used to a rich variety of entertainment: pageants, fairs, carnivals and markets, tournaments and jousts, court and wedding masques, royal progresses, religious processions, swordmanship exhibitions, the drilling of the local militia. There were travelling storytellers, mountebanks (tricksters like false healers who sold ineffective medicines in public), fortune-tellers, jugglers.

The tragedies of Shakespeare, Webster, Middleton and others reflected characters, emotions, actions and issues that were familiar to London audiences. In *The Duchess of Malfi*, Bosola, about to have the Duchess murdered, speaks words which refer to the custom of a bell being tolled at Newgate prison just before the execution of a condemned criminal:

> I am the common Bellman
> That usually is sent to condemn'd persons,
> The night before they suffer.

The growth of London – and the economic expansion of England as a whole – aided the development of the theatre. Between 1590–1620 English drama expanded spectacularly as playwrights, actors and theatres attracted audiences from all levels of society. Impoverished apprentices, servingmen, carters, porters, journeymen and workmen of all kinds stood in the theatre yards ('groundlings'). The more affluent paid to sit: aristocrats, politicians, university men, lawyers, merchants, soldiers and sailors, anyone who could afford the extra charges. Some even sat on the stage itself.

Gentlemen up from the country would take their wives to a play. Women from all social ranks were in the audience. For the many foreign visitors to London, a visit to the theatre was an essential part of their London experience, just as it is for tourists today. Such visits gave them something extra to talk about on their return home: the productions they had seen and the behaviour of the groundlings, wits and gentry, and others in the audience.

The audiences wanted entertainment, but such entertainment included the widest range of experience. There was coarse comedy and subtle wit, horrors and gentleness, love and enmity. Audiences witnessed scenes of violence and harmony, revenge and forgiveness. They heard all kinds of direct and indirect comments on affairs of state, law and belief. Whether the drama supported or subverted religious beliefs, traditional values or social organisation, it held attractions that pulled in the audiences. Each audience member could find something in the play they watched that confirmed or challenged their own perceptions and preferences.

In Shakespeare's lifetime, theatres and players became increasingly respectable, enjoying the patronage of aristocrats and wealthy citizens. Shakespeare's own company frequently performed at court, and in 1603 became The King's Men, an acknowledgement that they were the leading acting company in England. Queen Elizabeth and King James both enjoyed plays, frequently inviting various companies to play before them. But it was unthinkable that Queen Elizabeth would attend a public theatre (her visit in the film *Shakespeare in Love* is a delightful invention). Nonetheless many courtiers visited the playhouses, both to see and be seen.

But theatres were suspiciously regarded by the authorities. They were seen as breeding idleness and irreligion, taking students away from their studies, apprentices from their work, and good citizens from the church. Plays and players were distrusted, and seen as potentially subversive. Playhouses were places where society was subjected to examination and criticism. Theatres might display treason, blasphemy or libel on stage, and encourage their audiences to follow that example.

Theatre was looked upon as politically important. To aid their ineffective and ill-fated rebellion against Queen Elizabeth, supporters of the Earl of Essex paid Shakespeare's company to put on a production of *Richard II* with its scene of a king being deposed. The rebellion failed, and Shakespeare and his fellows were lucky to get off unscathed.

Tragedy especially exposed the conflicts in society. Its subject matter was potentially explosive, dealing as it did with state power, justice and crime. Tragedy examined the relationship between individual, state and religion. It could demystify state power and religion, showing them as serving sectional and personal interests rather than the whole community. For some in authority, tragedy dangerously implied there could be alternative, more radical, even egalitarian relationships in society.

It is therefore no wonder that playhouses were seen as fertile breeding grounds for dissent and riot. What was shown on their stages could challenge the authority of church and state. As a result, dramatists were sometimes harassed, imprisoned or otherwise punished. Powerful individuals or groups wanted to shut down theatres. In 1624, the Spanish ambassador complained about Middleton's *A Game at Chess*. The result was that the actors were arrested and the Globe was closed.

Not only might theatres present subversive ideas and so damage the political or religious status quo, they might also damage physical health. Up to 3000 citizens could squeeze in at the Globe – and where there were crowds, the plague could easily spread. Theatres were also associated with crime. They provided rich pickings for prostitutes and pickpockets.

So the theatre, potentially dangerous to social order, had to be curbed. A carefully constructed system of censorship and control developed. In 1581 the Master of the Revels was given commission to regulate and censor plays. It meant that acting companies had to submit plays for approval, in return for which they gained 'protection' of a sort. There were many other instances of control by either central or local authorities.

An Order of the Privy Council in 1600 declared that plays were 'the daily occasion of idle riotous and dissolute living of great numbers of people', giving rise to 'many particular abuses and disorders'. In 1606 an Act ordered a fine of £10 on anyone who 'in any stage-play, interlude, show, May-game, or pageant, jestingly or profanely speak or use the holy name of God, or of Jesus Christ, or of the Holy Ghost, or of the Trinity (which are not to be spoken but with fear and reverence)'. One result was that such oaths as 'Zounds (God's wounds) were cut in reprints of *Richard III*.

The very nature of theatre was suspect. It was intrinsically deceptive, a place for play acting, pretending, presenting things which were not true. Theatre dealt in disguise, artifice and deceit. It practised cross-dressing, and boys dressing as girls was against biblical teaching. For such practices, theatre came under fierce attack from Puritans who claimed that audiences risked eternal damnation, because plays, sin and the plague were utterly interlinked. In 1633, the Puritan William Prynne summed up 50 years of criticism of stage plays as 'sinful, heathenish, lewd, ungodly ... wicked, unchristian'.

▶ What is your own view of the political power of drama? Do you think the tragedies discussed in this book confirm or challenge authority (in Jacobean times and now)? Suggest how one or two of the tragedies you know might have political significance.

Everyday events, witchcraft

Jacobean revenge tragedies were often based on actual events in Italy or Spain. Shakespeare and the Jacobean playwrights made use of actual events in their own time as inspiration for plot development or to illuminate particular episodes. Contemporary audiences probably experienced a thrill of recognition as they heard particular passages spoken, or well-known issues or 'true stories' imaginatively evoked. For example, a line in *The Changeling* refers to scandalous gossip at the time as to how the Countess of Essex was physically examined to discover if she was a virgin (see page 67).

Macbeth contains references to the Gunpowder Plot of 1605 ('dire combustion and confused events'). In the Porter's talk of 'equivocation' audiences were probably reminded of the trial of Doctor Lopez for the planned assassination of

Queen Elizabeth. In that trial it was argued that a defendant could lie ('equivocate') in order to maintain his faith. Similarly, Cleopatra's fear that she will see, as a prisoner in Rome 'Some squeaking Cleopatra boy my greatness' clearly refers to the practice in Shakespeare's time of boy actors playing women.

Another theatrical example occurs in Hamlet's exchange with Rosencrantz and Guildenstern. Hamlet asks why the Players are forced to travel, and why their reputation ('estimation') has declined. He is told it is because of 'an eyrie of children, little eyases, that cry out on top of question' (a nest of child actors, as noisy as unfledged hawks). This was a company of boy players, very active around the time that Shakespeare was writing *Hamlet*, who enjoyed great success in London. For a short time these 'little eyases' threatened the livelihood of some adult professional acting companies which were forced to tour because they could not attract London audiences. The same episode in *Hamlet* is also thought to be about the 'wars of the theatres' in which the rivalry between adult companies led to intense mocking of each other, or 'much throwing about of brains' as Guildenstern describes it.

Perhaps the most striking contemporary reference is to the many witchcraft trials of the period. England was a superstitious society. For all the advances in science and knowledge, many people believed in omens and portents. Witches and witchcraft were the object of morbid and fevered fascination throughout the reign of Queen Elizabeth. Most people believed that witches existed, and persecution of those accused of witchcraft was widespread. Many suffered torture and death by burning.

The persecution continued when King James came to the throne in 1603. He was obsessed with witchcraft, and was convinced that Satan was always laying plots to destroy him, using witches as devilish agents. An Act of Parliament in 1604 decreed that anyone found guilty of practising witchcraft should be executed. It is possible that Shakespeare wrote *Macbeth* partly because of King James' obsession, and partly to draw in audiences who would relish seeing witches portrayed on stage.

Assignments

1 Shakespeare's fellow playwright, Ben Jonson, claimed that Shakespeare was 'not for an age, but for all time'. In contrast, this book is concerned to show that Shakespeare, like Webster and Middleton, was very much a man of his time. Can both views be true? What evidence would you use to argue that the tragedies reflect the preoccupations of the Elizabethan and Jacobean age, but also have universal appeal today?

2   'Something is rotten in the state of Denmark.' Marcellus' comment in *Hamlet* has often been interpreted as Shakespeare's comment on the state of England. Find some quotations from the tragedy you are studying that you think might be a veiled criticism of his society by the playwright. Justify each of your quotations in one or two sentences.

3   Look back through pages 15–38 and make your own summary of contexts and events that influenced Shakespeare and the Jacobeans as they wrote their tragedies. Then consider the tragedy you know best and suggest how each item on your list might be reflected in some way in the play.

4   In *Julius Caesar* and *Coriolanus*, the ordinary people of Rome play a significant part in the developing tragedy. In the Russian film of *King Lear* (1970), the director, Grigori Kozintzev, ensures that poor, starving people are a powerful presence. They are a constant reminder to the audience of the wretched plight of Lear's subjects. But in many tragedies, ordinary people rarely appear. Consider the tragedy you know best and suggest ways in which a film version might reflect the conditions and viewpoints of the poor. How far do you think such a version is justified?

5   Shakespeare and his Acting Company often performed at court before Queen Elizabeth or King James. Work in a group. Imagine you are Shakespeare and his fellow actors. You have been invited to play a tragedy before King James. You wish to use the opportunity to criticise James and his courtiers, but in ways which will not bring down anger and punishment. Choose your tragedy and discuss how you intend to present it. Which scenes and lines will you focus on?

6   Choose one tragedy and suggest how a Jacobean audience might have responded to it. How are those responses likely to be different from those of a modern audience?

3 | Approaching the texts

- Is each Shakespearean tragedy unique, or do all share common features?

- In what ways do Shakespeare's tragedies reveal the cultural and social conditions of their times?

- What are the major features of Jacobean tragedy?

- How do Jacobean tragedies reflect their times?

Shakespearean tragedy

Because Shakespeare was a playwright who was always restlessly experimenting throughout his career, many people think that it is preferable to speak of 'Shakespeare's tragedies' rather than 'Shakespearean tragedy'. They point to the sheer variety of the tragedies, and claim that every one is different. They argue that Shakespeare never repeated himself, and that each tragedy has a distinctiveness that sets it quite apart from the others. While there is a good deal of truth in such a view, there is a good case to be made that Shakespeare did 'repeat himself'. It is probably more helpful to accept that although every Shakespearean tragedy has its uniqueness, it also shares common features with other tragedies.

The most obvious common feature is 'tragedy': every play contains a tragic character (or characters) who suffers and dies; each play moves inexorably towards some kind of catastrophe. Similarly, every tragedy shows Shakespeare's preoccupation with particular issues or themes, for example, appearance and reality, conflict, change. In the same way, every tragedy is about 'loss' or 'waste': in each something precious is lost or wasted, most obviously, life itself, but also innocence or youth or honour and so on. The language of the tragedies also displays similarities, for example in the frequent use of imagery. But of course each play has its own particular story, characters, setting and language through which Shakespeare gives these common features unique and vivid expression.

All Shakespeare's tragedies also show evidence of being influenced by similar social and cultural aspects of his time. The various features of Elizabethan and Jacobean England set out in Part 2 (pages 15–38) can all be identified in many of the tragedies. Some are clearly present in every tragedy, although, of course, taking different form in each, for example, beliefs about women, hierarchy in society and nature, and religion. In addition, it is possible to identify what Shakespeare read that fired his imagination for each play; for example Plutarch's *Lives* was the source of at least four of his tragedies.

To study Shakespeare's tragedies in context, it is advisable to know as much as you can of the particularities of each play, and also to be aware of the features they have in common and how each is influenced by the conditions of the times. The following discussions of each tragedy will help your study of context. The plays are presented in chronological order, but the date given for each tragedy is only approximate (c.=*circa*, Latin for approximate), the one generally agreed by most Shakespearean scholars.

▶ How would you describe the difference between 'Shakespearean tragedy' and 'Shakespeare's tragedies'? How does that difference affect your study of the plays?

▶ Select one feature you think all Shakespeare's tragedies have in common (for example, exploring issues of 'loss', or 'appearance and reality'). Identify how that feature occurs in the tragedies you have studied.

Titus Andronicus (c. 1592)

Titus Andronicus is Shakespeare's first tragedy. Its violent, melodramatic nature shows the influence of Kyd's *The Spanish Tragedy* (see pages 17–19). Like Kyd's play, it was hugely successful in the theatre. Audiences responded enthusiastically to its blend of lyrical poetry with sensational horrors of rape, mutilation and cannibalism. Titus' description of Rome as 'a wilderness of tigers' expresses the barbarity of the patriarchal, racist and sexist society of the play.

The tragedy is powered by the desire to revenge, an impulse that fascinated contemporary audiences (see pages 10, 16–17). Tamora, Queen of the Goths, seeks to revenge her son who has been executed by Titus as a sacrifice for his own sons killed fighting the Goths. Her revenge is terrible, resulting in the execution of two of Titus' sons, his chopping off of his own hand, and worst of all, the rape and mutilation of his daughter Lavinia, whose hands and tongue are cut off. In return, Titus, denied justice because Tamora becomes Empress of Rome, remorselessly exacts his own revenge. He kills Tamora's sons who violated Lavinia, cooks them in a pie and feeds it to their mother, who he then slays. Revenge is quite literally an eye for an eye.

Titus suffers like a **tragic hero,** but Shakespeare leaves open the question whether he learns from that suffering. Lavinia is an innocent victim, but is killed by Titus at the end of the play because of the shame and dishonour he feels his daughter has brought upon him: 'Die, die, Lavinia, and thy shame with thee.' His action reflects a contemporary attitude towards women: even when blameless, their violation was a stain on male honour.

▶ In the 2000 film of *Titus Andronicus*, Antony Hopkins plays with great glee the scene in which Titus butchers and serves up Tamora's sons. Part of that scene is given in the extract on page 74. Read the extract, identify the features that make it tragic, then write notes to show how you would direct the episode on stage or on film.

Richard III (c. 1592–1593)

From the time of its first performance, *Richard III* was an immense popular success. No fewer than five editions of the play were published during Shakespeare's lifetime. On stage, Richard's combination of villainy and charm created compelling theatre. Shakespeare gave Richard a deformed body, but he also gave him the ability to attract and hold an audience. Richard dominates the play as a restless role-player, using cynical humour and candid asides to cover his malice and deceit as he murders his way to the throne of England.

What kind of play is *Richard III*? It is obviously a history, even though its portrayal of history is very questionable (Shakespeare was a playwright not an historian). But it is also a tragedy. In the First Folio of 1623 its title page describes it as *The Tragedy of Richard the Third*, and the play portrays the rise and fall, suffering and death of a deeply flawed high status character. Shakespeare however was developing his own unique style of tragedy, one in which comedy disrupts the sombre, serious atmosphere. In the first three Acts of *Richard III*, comedy is always close to the surface as Richard delights in his own deceitful behaviour.

Shakespeare's knowledge of tragedy, and his abiding interest in the theme of appearance and reality is evident in a speech he gives to the hypocritical Buckingham, who tells how he can deceive like an actor in a tragedy:

> I can counterfeit the deep tragedian,
> Speak and look back, and pry on every side,
> Tremble and start at wagging of a straw;
> Intending deep suspicion, ghastly looks
> Are at my service, like enforced smiles.

▶ Speak Buckingham's lines adding actions and expressions. Then consider each action Buckingham describes (there are at least six) and decide whether you think it is characteristic of an actor in tragedy.

Richard III arises out of its times. It may in part be Shakespeare's rewriting of an earlier play by an unknown author: *The True Tragedy of Richard III*. One indication of the censorship under which Shakespeare and his contemporaries worked is that the word 'Zounds ('By God's wounds', a mild oath) appears in early versions of the play, but was cut from the Folio version. This is almost certainly because of an Act of 1606 which forbade all mention of God's name on stage. There were other social, literary and dramatic contexts which influenced its writing:

- The defeat of the Spanish Armada in 1588 encouraged a great upsurge in interest in national identity. *Richard III* is one of a host of history plays that celebrated English, and particularly Tudor, achievements. It ends with a scene which would have especially pleased Queen Elizabeth as well as the English audiences: the establishment of the Tudor monarchy.

- The play shows Shakespeare's reading of history books which were concerned to establish the legitimacy of the Tudor dynasty. The *Chronicles* of Hall and Holinshed (see page 22) were based on Sir Thomas More's account of Richard. More portrayed Richard as an evil monster, twisted in mind and body, who brought great suffering to England until he was overthrown by Richmond, the first Tudor king, Henry VII. It was More's version of Richard that spread the rumour that Richard was 'born with teeth', a phrase that Shakespeare incorporates into the play.

- The play also displays the influence of Senecan tragedies that were popular around the time the play was written (see pages 16–17). The language is often ritualistic and stylised; Margaret is a kind of tragic chorus; ghosts of Richard's victims appear and variously bless Richmond and curse Richard; dreams afflict Clarence, Hastings and Richard himself. The play also portrays the working out of justice as Richard brings retribution down upon himself. He suffers and is finally killed for the wrongs he has committed (a process that Tudor historians saw as part of a divine plan: the working out of the will of God).

- Richard's character owes much to the sinister but comic Vice of medieval morality plays (see page 21), and to Machiavelli (see page 23). In the play, Richard likens himself to 'the formal Vice, Iniquity'. In an earlier play (*King Henry VI part 3*), he had claimed he would 'set the murderous machiavel to school'.

▶ Turn to the extract on pages 75–77 and work on one or more of the following:

Identify how Shakespeare uses some of the conventional devices of Senecan tragedy (see pages 16–17).

Compare Richard's soliloquy (beginning 'Give me another horse') with Hamlet's soliloquy ('To be or not to be') on page 80. What similarities and differences can you find? Which do you consider more dramatically and/or poetically effective? Give reasons for your choice.

Work out how to stage the extract to heighten the audience's sense of tragedy.

Richard II (c. 1594)

Richard II is a history play, but displays many of the features of tragedy. Richard's lament when he faces the prospect of losing his throne might well stand for

Shakespeare's conception of tragedy:

> For God's sake let us sit upon the ground
> And tell sad stories of the death of kings.
> How some have been deposed, some slain in war,
> Some haunted by the ghosts they have deposed,
> Some poisoned by their wives, some sleeping killed,
> All murdered.

Like *Richard III* and the other history plays, *Richard II* is part of a sequence of Shakespeare's account of the creation of England as nation state. He again uses the *Chronicles* of Holinshed as his main source, and portrays the fall of Richard as that of a flawed and ineffectual ruler, overthrown by the pragmatic Bullingbrook who becomes King Henry IV. Richard's suffering and death has strong Christian echoes, and he has been played as a Christ-like figure in some productions. The final scene in which Richard reflects 'I have wasted time, and now doth time waste me' before he is murdered can achieve great tragic intensity on stage.

The play deals with a controversial and explosive issue of Shakespeare's own time: is it right to depose a monarch, however evil or ineffectual? The question of how to live under a bad king, and how to prevent his tyranny, vices or foolishness, was hotly discussed in both Elizabeth's and James' reign. The authorities were acutely aware of the dangers that might come from any possibility of challenge to royal rule, and employed a host of controls to prevent active dissent.

Shakespeare dramatises the 'deposition' scene in which Richard is stripped of his powers and position as king. The ceremony with which Richard gives away his crown and all symbols of kingship would arouse very strong emotions in an Elizabethan or Jacobean audience:

> I give this heavy weight from off my head,
> And this unwieldy sceptre from my hand,
> The pride of kingly sway from out my heart.
> With mine own tears I wash away my balm,
> With mine own hands I give away my crown,
> With mine own tongue deny my sacred state,
> With mine own breath release all duteous oaths …

In many printed versions – and probably in performance – the deposition scene was omitted as too inflammatory. It might provoke thoughts of rebellion against the crown. Its relevance became all too clear in real life with the outbreak of the English Civil War in 1642, as a result of which King Charles I was deposed and beheaded.

The contemporary relevance of the play was not lost on Shakespeare's audience, or on the Queen herself. On one occasion Elizabeth remarked 'I am Richard II, know you not that?' Her sensitivity was heightened because she knew that, like Richard, she had favourite courtiers whose exploitation of England through their use of monopolies (see page 30) provoked furious anger against 'the caterpillars of the commonwealth' (the greedy courtiers who fed on England). The power of the deposition scene is evident in the fact that when followers of the Earl of Essex attempted to provoke a rebellion against Elizabeth, they paid Shakespeare's company to mount a production on the day of the rebellion. The uprising failed, and Shakespeare and his fellow actors were lucky to escape without punishment.

The tragic nature of the play is much concerned with the conflict that Richard experiences between his public role as king and his personal feelings. Shakespeare dramatises this conflict between what was known as 'the king's two bodies': the one as divine, God's representative on earth; the other as personal and private. Richard believes he has divine authority to rule:

> Not all the water in the rough rude sea
> Can wash the balm from an anointed king.

But his personality is sensitive and poetic, easily yielding to tears. Shakespeare gives him language to express these qualities, and so heighten the tragedy of his fall from king to powerless prisoner. Caught between his personal feelings and his obligations as king, Richard is ripe for overthrow by the less imaginative, more powerful Bullingbrook, a character more in tune with the sceptical thinking of Shakespeare's own times.

▶ Step into role as director of a stage production and describe how you would stage the seven lines from the deposition scene opposite to bring out their dramatic qualities as tragedy.

▶ Read the extract from *Richard II* on pages 77–78. Use it to argue that the 'tragic hero' of the play is England, rather than Richard.

Romeo and Juliet (c. 1595)

Romeo and Juliet are not the conventional characters of tragedy. They are young, have little or no power within their society, and are not members of the ruling family of Verona. But the play is accepted as a tragedy. Capulet's final line 'Poor sacrifices of our emnity' is often quoted to describe the play as a 'sacrificial tragedy': the young are sacrificed to bring about the end of the feud that splits Verona. Shakespeare was expanding traditional notions of tragedy to centre it on loss and waste, the senseless destruction of young love by the hostility of the families into which they had been born.

Shakespeare's Verona is a very different place from the Italy portrayed by Webster, Middleton and other playwrights. *Romeo and Juliet* does not portray the typically corrupt Italian court of Jacobean tragedy (see page 11), but it does reflect London life of the 1590s. Young men in gangs roam the streets looking for trouble. They are desperate to protect their territory and the honour of their clan. There is a servant who cannot read (illiteracy was widespread in Shakespeare's time). In the Capulet household, the servants gossip and the musicians crack weak jokes just as they did at English festivities. The Duke and the Friar resemble the secular and religious authorities of Elizabethan England.

Shakespeare's debt to other drama is clear. He uses the conventional characters of Italian comedy popular in his day: an earthy, talkative nurse; an angry father who wants his daughter to marry the man of his choice; an apothecary; a pair of lovers; an unwelcome lover; feuding families. Shakespeare's reading is also very evident. He found the idea for *Romeo and Juliet* in Arthur Brooke's poem 'The Tragical History of Romeus and Juliet', written in 1562. Shakespeare followed Brooke's plot closely, but used his skill as a dramatist to turn the dull poem into gripping theatre.

The language of the play also reflects the context of the times. During Queen Elizabeth's reign the Italian poet Petrarch (1304–1374) had become very popular with English poets. They drew on Petrarch's themes and style to write about courtly love. In the early 1590s virtually all poets were writing sonnets. Shakespeare was probably writing his own sonnets around the time he wrote the play. *Romeo and Juliet* contains several sonnets and other features of Petrarch's style: elaborate conceits (fanciful imagery), neat rhymes, and much witty word-play using repetition and puns. Such verbal fireworks appealed to audiences of the time. Romeo's love for Rosaline (who never appears in the play) echoes the major theme of Petrarch's poetry: a young man's unrequited love of a disdainful and unattainable woman. Romeo was infatuated with Rosaline, but she rejected all his advances.

▶ Read the extract on pages 78–79. Think about why Shakespeare deliberately makes Juliet only thirteen (much younger than the age at which most Elizabethans married), and suggest which characteristics of Juliet's language intensify the sense of tragedy.

Julius Caesar (c. 1599)

Shakespeare wrote *The Tragedy of Julius Caesar* about half way through his career as a dramatist. The play is often seen as the prelude to the great tragedies which were to follow. Shakespeare based the play on the version of Caesar's life he found in Sir Thomas North's translation (1579) of Plutarch's *The Lives of the Noble Grecians and Romans*.

Plutarch compares pairs of famous men, telling anecdotes about their lives to illustrate a moral or historical lesson. In Shakespeare's time, North's translation of Plutarch was very popular among educated people who believed they could learn valuable lessons from studying the lives of great men in the past. As was his usual practice, Shakespeare altered what he read to create gripping drama.

The Elizabethans had a great interest in Rome. A popular myth claimed that the English were descended from the Romans. More importantly, the story of Caesar raised questions that were hotly debated in Elizabethan England. Just as Brutus and Cassius feared that Caesar was trying to gain total power in the state, so too many English worried that Elizabeth, and even more so James, intended to become the sole, unquestioned ruler of the country. The elected House of Commons, although nothing like a modern democratic institution, contested the rights of the crown and sought to control the ambition and expenditure of the monarch.

At the time Shakespeare wrote the play, certain aspects of England paralleled those of Rome. Elizabeth had survived assassination attempts, but she was clearly coming to the end of her reign. She had no children, and the question of who would succeed her was by no means clear. Instability and civil war threatened. The tight censorship of the times meant that the question of who should next rule England could not be openly debated. But the theatre, although also subject to strict control, could provoke discussion and enable the question to be addressed indirectly. An English history play might well be censored, but the issues could be mirrored and explored in a play set in ancient Rome.

Once again, Shakespeare's own world is evident in the play. He imagines the characters wearing doublet and hose (and sweaty nightcaps!). A clock strikes, a sound unknown in Roman times, but familiar to the Elizabethans. The descriptions of the skyline of Rome is like that of Shakespeare's London: towers, roofs, windows, chimney tops. The Roman plebeians represented the dangerous London mobs that might overthrow established authority. Shakespeare also addresses other questions that puzzled his contemporaries, and which were increasingly rejected by more scientific and sceptical ways of thinking. For example, Cassius strongly rejects the claim that astrology determines human personality:

The fault, dear Brutus, is not in our stars
But in ourselves, that we are underlings.

Shakespeare might also be seen enjoying his own theatrical success in the scene where the conspirators wash their hands in Caesar's blood. Cassius' prophecy has been borne out in productions of the play for over 400 years:

> How many ages hence
> Shall this our lofty scene be acted over
> In states unborn and accents yet unknown!

The language of the play displays the rhetorical techniques Shakespeare had learned in his Stratford classroom. For example, as Brutus weighs up the arguments for killing Caesar, his style of considering both sides of the question is similar to the exercises that Shakespeare himself completed as a student. The question 'Was Brutus right or wrong in murdering Caesar?' had been set as an essay title in an educational book for 16th-century schoolboys by the Dutch scholar, Erasmus. But *Julius Caesar* shows that **rhetoric** is much more than a school exercise. It demonstrates the power of language to move a mob to action, to inflame, to provoke to murder and destruction. The Elizabethan authorities feared demagogues (rabble-rousers) with the skills of Antony.

▶ The title of the play is *Julius Caesar*. But many critics argue that Brutus is the 'tragic hero'. Make a list of the titles of as many tragedies as you can. How many refer directly to the 'hero' (main tragic character)? What thoughts do you imagine go through a playwright's head when he or she is deciding on a title for a tragedy?

Hamlet (c. 1601)

At the end of *Hamlet*, four dead bodies lie on the stage. Four other dead bodies lie elsewhere. Horatio's summary of the story he proposes to tell sounds like a description of the genre of 'revenge tragedy':

> So shall you hear
> Of carnal, bloody, and unnatural acts,
> Of accidental judgements, casual slaughters,
> Of deaths put on by cunning and forced cause,
> And in this upshot, purposes mistook
> Fallen on th'inventors' heads.

Hamlet contains many of the conventions of revenge tragedy (see pages 10, 17 and 19). A ghost demands revenge, but the revenger is unable to obtain justice because the killer is now the king. There are mad scenes and frequent expressions of contempt for the world. Revenge provokes revenge as Laertes seeks to avenge the death of his father Polonius, killed by Hamlet who mistakes him for Claudius. But with the creation of Hamlet, Shakespearean tragedy moves far beyond the blood-boltered melodramas of the early 1590s. Hamlet is a tragic hero who is unsure whether or not he should carry out his father's ghost's command to revenge.

The image of Hamlet contemplating the skull ('Alas poor Yorick!') may be the most famous in all drama. But it is more than simply a theatrical pose. It symbolises crucial aspects of human consciousness in Shakespeare's time: the preoccupation with individual identity, and the lack of certainty of what would happen after death. Hamlet's Denmark is like the England of Shakespeare's own time. It is a transitional society between an older world of feudalism and chivalry and an emerging modern world. In Shakespeare's England, medieval certainties were yielding to scepticism and doubt, as visions of alternative beliefs and lifestyles emerged:

- In religion, the growth of Protestantism undermined traditional belief, making individuals responsible for the state of their souls, yet less assured of what lay in store for them after death.

- In science, observation and experiment disproved the belief that human beings were at the centre of a fixed and stable cosmos.

- In exploration, the discovery of new worlds and cultures expanded belief that life might be lived in different ways (for example, without kings or social hierarchy).

- In economic life, increasing wealth and entrepreneurial activity offered possibilities for individuals to rise up the social hierarchy through their own efforts.

Such doubts and understandings are embodied in the character of Hamlet. His preoccupation with sin and salvation shows he is the product of a feudal world where religion was used as an instrument of control. But his style of thought marks him out as a self-conscious modern individual. Hamlet is the most 'inward' of all Shakespeare's tragic heroes (indeed, of all Shakespeare's characters). He continually debates with himself. He questions what he sees, hears and thinks, and in a series of soliloquies he opens his thoughts and feelings to searching examination by himself and by the audience. That 'inwardness' is most evident in his 'To be or not to be' soliloquy (see page 80).

Hamlet is also one of the most contradictory of Shakespeare's tragic characters. He can speak great poetry, yet he can revile a young woman, stab her father in a moment of sudden violence, and send two old friends to their death without a twinge of conscience. In one speech, Hamlet describes a tragic flaw: 'some vicious mole in nature', 'the stamp of one defect'. His own tragic flaw may be that he thinks too much, or, as Laurence Olivier's film puts it 'This is the tragedy of a man who cannot make up his mind'. He is a revenger who is prevented from action by his own thoughts.

There is space to mention only a few other ways in which *Hamlet* can be seen to arise out of the times in which it was written. It mirrors the anxieties of Shakespeare's England. Claudius' murder of Old Hamlet was a political assassination to achieve political power. Both Elizabeth and James were subject to assassination attempts. Polonius may be modelled on Lord Burghley, who also believed in close surveillance to maintain order. Just as Burghley maintained an extensive network of spies, so Polonius is infected by the same desire to overhear in secret, to keep all potential dissidents under surveillance. He spies on Hamlet and he sends Reynaldo to spy on Laertes, his own son.

Shakespeare drew upon religious beliefs current in his day. Suicides were believed to go straight to hell. Those who had not made full confession of their sins were believed to go to purgatory, where they suffered until their unconfessed sins were burnt away ('purged'). Such beliefs help explain events in the play. Ophelia is denied the full rites of Christian burial because the priest thought she had taken her own life. Hamlet refrains from killing Claudius at prayer for fear of sending him direct to heaven. His own father had been killed at a moment when he was unprepared for heaven, and now Old Hamlet suffers torments in purgatory. So Hamlet sheathes his sword and decides to wait, to catch Claudius at a moment 'That has no relish of salvation in't' (when there is no hope of Claudius' soul going to heaven).

Hamlet richly displays Shakespeare's interest in the theatre. There are many references to playing and acting, and the play resonates with dramatic images and language: 'show', 'perform', 'prologue', 'part'. Hamlet sees the purpose of acting as holding 'the mirror up to nature', to portray the nature of society: 'to show virtue her own feature, scorn her own image, and the very age and body of the time his form and pressure'. *Hamlet* does just that in many ways, as it reveals the contexts, particular and general, of its time.

▶ Work in pairs on the extract on page 80. Speak the soliloquy as a conversation, one person speaking a short section and the other 'replying' with the next short section, and so on. How far do the lines sound like a man debating with himself as a kind of internal conversation?

Othello (c. 1604)

Othello contains expression of the prejudices, the racial and sexual anxieties, towards blacks in Shakespeare's time. The slave trade had begun and was contributing to the wealth of English 'adventurers' (a polite term for those who exploited any commercial opportunity). A few blacks were seen on London streets, usually servants. They were regarded at best as exotic, interestingly strange, but more usually as potentially 'savage': threatening and dangerous. The thought of interracial marriage was abhorrent to most English men and women of the time. Iago uses ugly racist language: 'thick-lips', 'old black ram', and even the Duke's praise of Othello as 'far more fair than black' reveals how the Jacobeans regarded 'black' as associated with evil.

The play has compelling dramatic intensity. The dominant theme of jealousy, the small cast and tight timescale, all contribute to the headlong pace of the developing tragedy. It is generally regarded as Shakespeare's most domestic tragedy, a study of the personal psychology of Othello, Iago and Desdemona, rather than a political tragedy. The Venetian state is unaffected by Othello's fall. There are no kings or princes: even though Othello claims royal ancestors, he is a soldier who was once sold into slavery. There is only the briefest hint of the supernatural (in Othello's description of the handkerchief) and the play seems to concentrate on the human emotions which destroy love: sexual jealousy, hate and anger, ambition and ingratitude.

Although the play may not seem to be about politics, its presentation of Othello as black and older than Desdemona clearly raises crucial issues of race, age and culture. In the 20th century the play proved a significant symbol in the struggle for black emancipation. A long running American production in 1943 included the first ever kiss on stage between a black man and a white woman. All later productions in America commented with varying directness on the Civil Rights movement for equality between races. Similarly, in South Africa, a famous production at the Market Theatre, Johannesburg became a potent focus for the anti-apartheid campaign. Iago was portrayed as an intolerant Afrikaaner and Othello was played by a township black. Today fierce debate rages as to whether only a black man should play Othello. A 1999 production in Washington found a solution by casting a white actor as Othello and having every other character played by black actors.

Othello is an outsider in Venetian society, and his tragedy has been given even greater significance in modern times because of heightened awareness of racial issues. But the language of the play has always been part of its universal appeal. Othello's language ranges from the soaring operatic quality of some of his speeches

> O now forever
> Farewell the tranquil mind! Farewell content!
> Farewell the plumed troops, and the big wars
> That makes ambition virtue – O farewell!

to the simple and reflective

> Put out the light, and then put out the light

The imagery uses the natural world as a source of disturbing images of blind desires: goats and monkeys, baboons, wolves and spiders, flies, toads and dogs, asses, sheep, horses, serpents, guinea hens. Jealousy is 'the green-eyed monster', the poison that takes over Othello through the cunning malice of Iago.

Iago is yet another example of how Shakespeare used the Vice or machiavel character of older morality plays (see page 21). He also resembles the malcontents of Jacobean tragedy. Passed over for promotion, envious of Cassio, misogynistic (hating women), suspicious that his wife has been unfaithful to him with Othello, he seems to take perverse pleasure in poisoning Othello's mind and bringing about the death of the innocent Desdemona.

▶ Read the extract on pages 81–82. What clues can you find in the language that suggest Othello is a 'tragic hero' and Iago is a 'Vice' or 'machiavel'? Describe what you think is the relationship of the two men in this episode.

▶ How far do you think *Othello* presents a case for a society free of racial prejudice?

King Lear (c. 1605)

Two versions of *King Lear* exist. A Quarto version was published in 1608, in which the play was described as a 'history'. The Folio version was published in 1623, which titled the play *The Tragedy of King Lear*. The Folio is now thought to be Shakespeare's final revision of the play for stage performance, heightening the tragic atmosphere, making it more sombre and bleak, creating a world in which the gods are malicious or simply indifferent to humanity's fate.

King Lear may be a comment on the hierarchy of the Jacobean state, on **patriarchy,** and on King James' belief in his divine right to rule. Lear, once all-powerful, gives away his kingdom to his daughters, but still wants unquestioning love and absolute obedience from them. But his two daughters Gonerill and Regan abuse him cruelly. He falls from the condition of king to that of the most wretched beggar, and on the heath he experiences a vision of humanity at its lowest and most elemental: 'the thing itself – poor unaccommodated man'. After much suffering, he acknowledges that he has 'taken too little care' of the suffering of the poor, and he learns the value of love and forgiveness, expressed through his youngest daughter Cordelia whom he had angrily banished at the start of the play.

Many critics believe *King Lear* to be the supreme example of Shakespeare's tragic genius, but, as the preceding paragraph implies, are sharply divided about the nature and causes of the tragedy. Jonathan Dollimore (1989) sees it as about society, describing it as 'above all, a play about power, property and inheritance'. In such a reading, Lear, Poor Tom and the Fool, as outcasts in their wretchedness on the heath, become symbols of the alienated and dispossessed of Jacobean society. In contrast, many other critics see the play as essentially a personal tragedy, about Lear's journey to redemption. For example G K Hunter argues that it is the greatest of Shakespeare's tragedies because

... it not only strips and reduces and assaults human dignity, but because it also shows with the greatest force and detail the process of restoration by which humanity can recover from degradation.

Whatever view critics take of the play there is agreement that it reveals much about the contemporary contexts which shaped the play in Shakespeare's imagination. Here are just a few:

- Shakespeare may have been thinking of the political anxieties that characterised the end of Queen Elizabeth's reign and the beginning of King James I's reign. There were fears of civil war and of the kingdom being divided.

- He may have seen an old play *The True Chronicle History of King Leir*, first performed in the 1590s, published in 1605. No characters die in the play, but it contains the stage direction of 'thunder and lightning' which may have been Shakespeare's inspiration for the storm.

- He may have heard the legendary story of Lear, first told in Geoffrey of Monmouth's *History of England*, written 400 years before Shakespeare's time.

- He may have read a retelling of that story in *A Mirror for Magistrates*, a collection of tragic tales drawn from the Bible, classical writers, legend, myth and history. Written in verse, the stories portray the unreliability of fortune, the suffering and fall of famous men and women, and the punishment of wrongdoers. Or he may have read it in Holinshed's *Chronicles* (see page 22) which told of King Leir and his three daughters, Gonorilla, Regan and Cordeilla.

- He certainly read a pamphlet, Samuel Harsnett's 'A Declaration of Egregious Popish Impostures' (1603). Much of Edgar's strange language when pretending to be Poor Tom is taken from this anti-Catholic pamphlet – especially the list of demon's names.

- He read a prose romance, 'Arcadia', a story by Sir Philip Sidney (1590), from which he took the Gloucester sub-plot of a father with two sons, one good, one bad.

- He may have been inspired by contemporary gossip and scandal about fathers and daughters. For example, Sir William Allen, a former Lord Mayor of London, split his estate between his three daughters and arranged to live alternately with each. But all three treated him cruelly and disrespectfully. Another popular subject of gossip in 1603–1604 was Sir Brian Annesley. His youngest daughter Cordell defended him against her eldest sister, who tried to have her aged father certified mad so that she could take control of his estate and wealth.

▶ Read the extract on pages 83–84. Work out different ways of staging it to express the interpretations of Dollimore and Hunter above (i.e. a 'social' tragedy emphasising power and wealth; and a 'personal' tragedy emphasising the personal feelings of the characters). Pages 117–118 can help you.

Macbeth (c. 1606)

Macbeth is hugely popular today, studied by millions of school students and frequently performed. Yet it is very much a play of its time, deeply rooted in the Jacobean England of the early years of the reign of King James I. Macbeth's severed head at the end of the play might be a chilling reminder to Shakespeare's audience of the heads of traitors displayed on pikes at each end of London Bridge, but the play also reflects many of James' interests:

*   Witchcraft
    The witches appear only three times in the play, but their presence is compellingly felt throughout the tragedy. They are often interpreted as reflecting James' obsessive fascination with witchcraft. He believed witches were plotting to kill him, attended witchcraft trials, and wrote a book on witchdraft, *Demonology*. When James became King of England in 1603 he ordered its immediate printing in London.

*   The divine right of kings (and regicide: the murder of a monarch)
    James was convinced that kings were divinely appointed by God. For him, that meant he had absolute power to rule as God's deputy on earth. The murder of Duncan would appal James who saw the killing of a king as a crime against God. James' father and mother had both been assassinated, and he lived in fear of the same fate.

*   The Gunpowder Plot, 5 November 1605
    A medal was struck to commemorate the king's escape from the planned assassination. It portrayed a snake concealed by flowers (in the play Lady Macbeth says 'Look like th'innocent flower but be the serpent under't'). The Plot may be referred to in the play (as 'dire combustion'), significantly shortly after Duncan's murder – an act of regicide. One of the Gunpowder Plot conspirators was Edward Digby, a favourite of the king. It is possible that the treacherous thane of Cawdor (a man in whom Duncan had 'absolute trust') is Shakespeare's representation of Digby.

*   Equivocation (telling deliberately misleading half truths) is a major theme of the play
    The truthfulness of the witches is always in question; the Porter jokes about an equivocator; Macbeth grows to doubt 'th'equivocation of the fiend that lies like truth'. In 1606 a Catholic priest, Father Henry Garnet, was accused of treason for involvement in the Gunpowder Plot. At his trial much was made of the fact that he

had written a book, *A Treatise on Equivocation*, which defended the right to give misleading answers in the interest of conscience.

- Banquo
  Shakespeare used Holinshed's *Chronicles* as his major source for *Macbeth* (see page 22). Holinshed included a detailed family tree of the Stuart dynasty showing King James' direct descent from Banquo (a totally fictional figure – he never existed!). In the apparitions scene, Shakespeare includes the stage direction 'A show of eight kings, and the last with a glass in his hand, Banquo's Ghost following'. James was the ninth Stuart king, and there is a theatrical story that when Shakespeare's company performed before King James in 1606 at Hampton Court, the 'glass' (mirror) was held up to reflect James. There is no documentary evidence for this story, but it does seem likely that the presentation of Banquo was designed to please James. In Holinshed, Banquo helps Macbeth murder Duncan. But Shakespeare lays full responsibility on the Macbeths alone, showing Banquo as true and honest.

- Honours
  At the end of the play Malcolm's gift of earldoms to his thanes reflects King James' liberal giving of English titles to his Scottish supporters (see page 29).

▶ In tragedy the central character (the 'tragic hero') is complex, revealing many changes of mood and thought. Read the extract on pages 85–86 and identify the different emotions and aspects of character that Macbeth expresses.

Antony and Cleopatra (c. 1606)

Antony and Cleopatra, described as a tragedy in the First Folio, shows Shakespeare at his most expansive. Whereas *Macbeth* is compressed and tightly focused, this play seems to sprawl across place and time. Shakespeare ignores the classical unities (conventions of playwriting that demanded unity of action, time and place, that is, drama with no sub-plots, all its events taking place within 24 hours, and set in a single location), and develops a much looser form. The 42 scenes move between Egypt and Rome. There are sea and land battles around the Mediterranean world, a host of characters, and constantly changing moods, with comedy or sexual innuendo often dominating. The sense of tragedy seems to arrive late in the play, with the bungled suicide of Antony and, later, Cleopatra's magnificent scene as she prepares for death.

Shakespeare constantly invites comparison and contrast between Egypt and Rome, East and West. Cleopatra and her world are female and exciting, dangerously given to pleasure and excess. It is a frivolous, sexualised world. But it is also colonised and available, a conquered world where the victors can revel in the pleasures of the flesh.

In contrast, Rome is masculine and military. It is a sober, austere world that looks with disapproval on Cleopatra as embodying vice and corruption (in the very first speech of the play, she is called 'gypsy' and 'strumpet'). Antony has 'gone native' and his delight in Egypt's pleasures sharply contrasts with Octavius' controlled and austere manner.

As with his other Roman plays, Shakespeare followed the story he found in Sir Thomas North's translation of Plutarch's *Lives* (see page 22). It is less easy than with *Macbeth* to relate *Antony and Cleopatra* to the politics of the Jacobean world, but there is a possibility that Octavius' final victory may be an oblique criticism of how King James also tried to take all political power into his own hands. A few contemporary references are clear, most notably in Cleopatra's fear that as a captive in Rome she will see a young male actor mockingly impersonate her: 'Some squeaking Cleopatra boy my greatness'. The image recalls the boy actors who played female roles in Shakespeare's time.

▶ Cleopatra's preparation for death is regarded as one of the greatest scenes in all tragedy. Read the extract on pages 87–88 and make a list of the qualities which make it so highly regarded as tragedy. Then step into role as director and work out how you would stage it to maximise dramatic effect.

Coriolanus (c. 1607)

Shakespeare used his knowledge and experience of his own times as he wrote *Coriolanus*. Like Coriolanus' Rome, in Shakespeare's England the great majority of the people were very poor: it was a land of 'haves' and 'have nots'. These two groups, one tiny, the other numerous, were the counterparts of Rome's patricians and plebeians: the powerful and the powerless.

In England's acutely hierarchical society, King James and the aristocracy clung to their privileges. They were obsessed with notions of honour and esteem, measured by rank, breeding and wealth.

The power and right to rule of England's small elite was increasingly challenged, particularly in the growing disaffection of the landless labourers who faced a lifetime of ceaseless toil and grinding poverty. They had virtually no control over their lives. In peace, famine was an ever present threat. In times of war, like Coriolanus' plebeians, they could be recruited into the army.

All of the following contemporary events have been claimed to influence Shakespeare as he wrote *Coriolanus*, portraying the antagonism of the plebeians and patricians:

• Enclosures and corn riots
Increasingly throughout Shakespeare's lifetime, land which had once been common was 'enclosed': claimed as the sole property of rich landlords. The

enclosures resulted in a huge underclass of labourers who possessed no land and whose misery was made worse by falling wages and rising prices.

Following a series of bad harvests, riots broke out in 1607–1608 in the English Midlands against enclosures and the hoarding of corn by 'gentlemen'.

Shakespeare was himself a gentleman and landowner in Warwickshire. He would have had first-hand knowledge of these uprisings, which find their echoes in Act I of *Coriolanus*, as the 'mutinous citizens' protest against the hoarding of corn by the patricians.

- The warrior-heroes of the time

  Some critics argue that Coriolanus is a portrait of Robert Devereux (1566–1601), Earl of Essex, a favourite of Queen Elizabeth. He was executed in 1601 for rebellion against the Queen. Others claim that Shakespeare had in mind Sir Walter Ralegh (1554–1618), another favourite of the Queen, and a rival of Essex. Ralegh held a monopoly of the tin mines in Cornwall, and there is much evidence that his exploitation made him hated by the miners and other ordinary citizens. He was famous for his pride and his delight in war.

  Perhaps Shakespeare was also fascinated by the challenge of portraying battle scenes on stage.

- Crown versus Parliament

  The conflict between the patricians and the tribunes in *Coriolanus* reflects the often bitter struggles for political power between King James and the House of Commons. The Commons appealed to their right as the popular voice of the people, and contested the king's assertion that by the will of God (divine right) he held the ultimate power to approve or reject laws. King James was deeply angered by the challenge to his authority and in 1605 contemptuously dismissed the Members of Parliament as 'the Tribunes of the people, whose mouths cannot be stopped'. In another echo of the play, one faction of the Commons wanted the argument with the king to be conducted 'mildly', a word Shakespeare uses to great effect in the play.

- King versus the City of London

  Coriolanus has also been seen as mirroring the antagonism between King James and the City of London over the right to levy taxation.

- Shakespeare's mother

  Was the play linked with the death of Shakespeare's mother in 1608? Her death may have prompted Shakespeare to write a play that explores the relationship of mother and son.

Shakespeare once again used a story he found in Plutarch's *Lives of the Noble Grecians and Romans* (see page 22). His dramatic imagination was fired by certain phrases and events in the *Lives*. Shakespeare followed Plutarch's 'Life of Caius Martius Coriolanus' closely, but he made all kinds of revisions to story and character, selecting and shaping in order to increase dramatic effect. He omits some events and invents others. He compresses historical events and greatly expands the roles of Menenius, Aufidius and the Tribunes.

Where Plutarch stresses that Coriolanus' character was affected by neglect after his father's death, Shakespeare emphasises the crucial importance of Volumnia in shaping his personality. In Plutarch, Coriolanus has two children. Shakespeare gives him only one. He makes the plebeians more dramatically lively than in Plutarch.

He turns Aufidius into a life-long rival of Coriolanus. Plutarch blames usury (money-lending at high rates of interest) as the prime cause of the plebeians' rebelliousness, but Shakespeare makes the main grievance the hoarding of corn by the patricians. At certain points in the play, Shakespeare follows Plutarch's prose very closely indeed.

▶ In the following lines of verse, Coriolanus (Caius Martius) speaks to his great enemy, Aufidius. Carefully compare Shakespeare's language with what he read in Plutarch and identify what changes he made to increase the dramatic intensity of the episode. Give your views on the changes and whether you think Shakespeare can be accused of plagiarism (stealing other people's writings).

> My name is Caius Martius, who hath done
> To thee particularly and to all the Volsces
> Great hurt and mischief; thereto witness may
> My surname, Coriolanus. The painful service,
> The extreme dangers, and the drops of blood
> Shed for my thankless country are requited
> But with that surname – a good memory
> And witness of the malice and displeasure
> Which thou shouldst bear me.
>
> (Shakespeare)

> I am Caius Martius, who hath done to thyself particularly, and to all the Volsces generally, great hurt and mischief, which I cannot deny for my surname of Coriolanus that I bear. For I never had other benefit nor recompense, of all the true and painful service I have done, and the extreme dangers I have been in, but this only surname; a good memory and witness, of the malice and displeasure thou shouldst bear me.
>
> (Plutarch)

Timon of Athens (c. 1608)

'Bitter', 'bleak', 'negative', 'cynical', 'disillusioned', 'jaundiced', 'dispiriting'. All these adjectives have been used to describe *Timon of Athens*. The play tells the story of a rich man who is overwhelmingly generous, borrowing money to throw lavish parties and shower his flattering friends with gifts. But when Timon is pressed to repay his debts, he finds he has no money, and his friends refuse to help him. Their ingratitude transforms him into a misanthrope (hater of mankind). He leaves Athens and lives in the woods, cursing and reviling all humanity. Finally, he makes his tomb beside the sea and dies.

Shakespeare once again used Plutarch's *Lives* (see page 22) as inspiration for the play, but seems to have left the play as an unfinished draft. Many theories exist about why Shakespeare did not return to the play, and one explanation is firmly rooted in the context of the times: it was too dangerous! The play precisely mirrors the financial condition of many Jacobean aristocrats. They too had borrowed heavily, mortgaging their land to finance their lavish lifestyles. Relying on credit, they bought all the latest luxuries that developing overseas trade had brought to England, dressed in sumptuous clothes, and entertained extravagantly with masques, banquets, hunting and spectacular shows of wealth. Many of the nobility had huge debts.

In this climate of conspicuous consumption, King James was the most prodigal spender, handing out expensive gifts to his favourites. So it is possible that Shakespeare thought his play to be so explosively critical of the king and aristocracy, that he put *Timon* to one side as a draft. Like the Poet and Painter in the play, Shakespeare and his fellow playwrights depended on the patronage of royalty and the nobility. To offend them by exposing their extravagance and debt could have unfortunate consequences.

▶ *Timon of Athens* is, like *King Lear*, much concerned with ingratitude. What similarities can you find in the extracts from the two tragedies on pages 83 and 89?

▶ Unlike nearly all other tragic heroes, Timon leaves the stage to die unseen. Compile a list of how other tragic figures die. What conclusions can you draw from your list?

Jacobean tragedy

Jacobean tragedy is often called 'revenge tragedy', or 'the tragedy of blood'. Any label can be misleading, because, like 'detective stories' or 'cowboy films', the genre contains many very different examples. But a common feature of almost all Jacobean tragedies is the desire for revenge. In every play, a character (or many characters, nearly always male) passionately seeks to avenge a wrong. He feels the wrong as a dishonour, and sees revenge as a duty that he owes to his family or to his honour. The play dramatises the quest for revenge, and shows how it results in multiple killings. Two lines from John Ford's *'Tis Pity She's a Whore* (c. 1629) speak for all the revengers of Jacobean tragedy:

> Revenge is all the ambition I aspire;
> To that I'll climb or fall: my blood's on fire

These violent and bloody plays held immediate relevance for the Jacobeans. They related to questions which directly affected their lives, and which were hotly debated: justice, lawlessness, honour, and the corruption and tyranny of political power. In addition, the tragedies expressed a dominant mood of the period. Pessimism and despair were fuelled by economic depression and social unrest. Religious and political conflict created a climate of unease and doubt, as old certainties of knowledge and belief were increasingly challenged. The tragedies' preoccupation with physical, moral and spiritual decay reflected similar anxieties felt by the Jacobeans, fearful for what would happen to them after death.

Jacobean tragedy has been likened to a visit to the Chamber of Horrors at Madame Tussaud's. It puts on stage a ghoulish, nightmare world, and appeals to the same fascination with violence and the bizarre as do many modern films. Jacobean playwrights were not squeamish in portraying gory details: fingers or hands are chopped off; poisoned skulls, books or portraits kill those who kiss them; victims are mentally tortured with shows of madmen or waxworks of their dead children.

The tragedies portray Catholic Italy and Spain as fantasy lands in which pride, greed and lust are rampant. Noblemen are violent and dissolute, tormented and destroyed by sexual passion. Women are either innocent victims or sensual and self-willed; the cause of the crimes the men commit. Such caricatures fed the ignorance and prejudice of many Jacobeans who saw foreign countries as degenerate and corrupt, their courts full of treachery, intrigue and sexual licence. But it is also possible that these foreign settings were an indirect way of criticising King James' court. Shakespeare's Sonnet 129 may have been written well before King James came to the throne, but it vividly expresses the spirit of Jacobean tragedy's obsession with how sexual appetite overwhelms social convention and leads to destruction:

> Th'expense of spirit in a waste of shame
> Is lust in action, and till action, lust
> Is perjured, murd'rous, bloody, full of blame,
> Savage, extreme, rude, cruel, not to trust,
> Enjoyed no sooner but despised straight,

Past reason hunted, and no sooner had,
Past reason hated as a swallowed bait
On purpose laid to make the taker mad:
Mad in pursuit, and in possession so,
Had, having, and in quest to have, extreme,
A bliss in proof, and proved, a very woe,
Before, a joy proposed, behind, a dream.
All this the world well knows, yet none knows well,
To shun the heaven that leads men to this hell.

▶ Think about the Jacobean tragedy you know best. Which character might most appropriately speak Sonnet 129? In what ways does it express what happens in the play?

There is much scholarly debate over the authorship of Jacobean tragedies. Playwrights certainly co-operated, and it was common practice for one writer to contribute a scene or episode to another writer's play (as Shakespeare did in a play called *Sir Thomas More*). But today, the outstanding writers of Jacobean tragedy are judged to be John Webster (c. 1578–1632) and Thomas Middleton (1580–1627). Webster's *The White Devil* and *The Duchess of Malfi*, and Middleton's *The Revenger's Tragedy*, *The Changeling* and *Women Beware Women* are acknowledged as the supreme examples of the genre of Jacobean revenge tragedy. (*The Revenger's Tragedy* was for long thought to be written by Cyril Tourneur, but most critics now regard Middleton as the author.) All five plays enjoy high critical and theatrical status and are frequently performed

In the film *Shakespeare in Love*, John Webster appears as a creepy young boy who tortures mice and who enjoys the killings in *Romeo and Juliet*. This unpleasant portrayal is based on the popular conception of Webster as a dramatist of gruesome imagination, morbidly obsessed by violence, suffering and death. Two 20th-century poets have provided memorable descriptions of Webster's plays. Rupert Brooke saw them as 'full of the feverish and ghastly turmoil of a nest of maggots', and T S Eliot's poem 'Whispers of Immortality' begins:

Webster was much possessed by death
And saw the skull beneath the skin

The White Devil (c. 1612)

Webster's play is based on actual events in 1576–1585 that fascinated and scandalised Europe. Vittoria Accoramboni, a beautiful but poor woman, married a minor courtier, but soon began an affair with a richer man, Orsini, Duke of

Bracciano. He had Vittoria's husband murdered, killed his own wife and secretly married Vittoria. The couple incurred the displeasure of the Pope and were forced to flee to Lake Garda. There the Duke died, Vittoria was murdered on the orders of her husband's relatives, and the murderers were themselves executed.

Webster drew upon many sources as he wrote. He used letters and gossip of the time, but changed the names, altered actual events (the real Duke died from overeating, Webster has him poisoned), and adjusted the morality of characters to fit his dramatic purposes (the Duke's wife becomes noble and faithful). He invented events like Flamineo's mock death, which is always a successful dramatic episode in the theatre, and introduced incidents from other stories and plays. For example, there are many echoes of Shakespeare, and a 'mad scene' in the play is generally accepted to be inspired by the Ophelia scenes in *Hamlet*. The fact that the play arose out of the literary context of its times is shown in the preface, in which Webster acknowledges the influence of other Jacobean playwrights: Chapman, Jonson, Beaumont, Fletcher – and Shakespeare.

The play that Webster fashioned from his sources and his imagination is a complex tale of intrigue and revenge. The Duke of Brachiano falls in love with Vittoria Corombona. But he is already married to Isabella. Flamineo, Vittoria's brother, helps Brachiano get rid of Isabella and Vittoria's husband. Flamineo also kills his own brother, watched by their mother who goes mad with grief. Vittoria is accused of murder and adultery, sentenced to imprisonment, but is rescued by Brachiano who then marries her. Isabella's brother, Francisco, Duke of Florence, determines to revenge his sister's murder, and his agents cruelly kill Brachiano. Flamineo demands his reward from Vittoria and she tries to kill him, but both are killed by Francisco's agents.

Webster makes use of the literary conventions of the time. Flamineo is malcontent (see page 25), machiavel (see page 23) and Vice (see page 21). Other characters represent 'humours' (see page 103): Brachiano is the choleric man, Francisco the phlegmatic man and so on. But Webster's portrayal of Vittoria breaks free of stereotypes, and on stage she comes over as a fully realised human being, resourceful, intelligent and brave. She defends herself at her trial with eloquence and wit, defiantly facing her accusers.

The title of the play expresses the Jacobeans' preoccupation with religion and with reality and appearance. Deceitful hypocrites are 'whited sepulchres', outwardly beautiful and good, but inwardly evil. Most critics think that the 'white devil' is Vittoria, a character who combines criminality with courage, and wins sympathy from the audience. But other characters also embody the deceit implied by the title: Brachiano, Flamineo, or the Cardinal. Webster's obsession with how magnificent display ('Glories') conceals emptiness within is revealed in two lines that occur in both *The White Devil* and *The Duchess of Malfi*:

Glories, like glow-worms afar off shine bright,
But looked too near have neither heat nor light.

It has been argued that the 'white devil' may not be an individual, but the whole
world of the court. Such an interpretation sees the play as Webster's savage
criticism of the court of King James. The fictional Italian court is like the English
court, where untrustworthy flattering courtiers plot against each other, and sexual
licence prevails. In the play 'great men' are referred to as 'violent thunder',
'whirlpools', 'wolves', 'eagles' and 'devils'. Such noblemen are full of evil desires:

There's but three furies found in spacious hell,
But in a great man's breast three thousand dwell

In this tragedy of political intrigue, the words Vittoria speaks just before her death
could be criticism of the perils of life at the court of King James:

O happy they that never saw the court,
Nor ever knew great men but by report.

▶ Read the extract on pages 90–91 (which includes a reference to the zoo in the
Tower of London in Jacobean times). Describe your feelings about how Vittoria and
Flamineo face their deaths. Which lines appeal to you most for their imaginative
and dramatic impact? Why?

The Duchess of Malfi (c. 1614)

The Duchess of Malfi, a widow, is warned by her brothers, the Cardinal and Duke
Ferdinand, not to re-marry. But she falls in love with her steward, Antonio, and
secretly marries him. The brothers, obsessively jealous about their high status and
hoping to inherit the Duchess' wealth, suspect her. They set Bosola, an escaped
galley slave, to spy on her. By offering fresh apricots which make her sick, Bosola
discovers the Duchess is pregnant. Fearful of discovery, the Duchess and Antonio
separate and flee. But she and her children are captured, and she is cruelly
tormented and then murdered. Her courage impresses Bosola, who becomes
conscience-stricken and remorseful, and develops a loathing for the Duke and the
Cardinal. Knowing they seek to destroy him, Bosola determines on revenge, but
kills Antonio by mistake. Duke Ferdinand goes insane, imagining himself a wolf.
Bosola kills the Cardinal, is himself slain by the mad Ferdinand, but lives long
enough to see Ferdinand killed by Antonio's friends.

The sense of tragedy arises from Webster's portrayal of the Duchess as an
obviously good person. That such an innocent and moral woman should unjustly

suffer and die heightens her tragic status.

The story is based on an actual event in which a Spanish princess was imprisoned because of her secret love. But it also reflects an actual happening in England in Webster's time. After years of marriage, Penelope, sister of the Earl of Essex, fell in love with Charles Blount, went to live with him and had children by him. Essex, a jealous brother, revealed their liaison in his confession made in 1601 just before he was executed (see pages 36 and 45). As a result, Penelope was confined to house-imprisonment. She was later released, but because she secretly married Blount, was forbidden from attending the court.

The play reflects many of the interests of the Jacobeans. Galileo's invention of the telescope is mentioned, but more significantly all kinds of things that fascinated Webster's contemporaries find expression in the tragedy:

- social class mobility – Antonio, a commoner, marries into the nobility

- macabre scenes of torment and death – the Duchess is shown a waxwork of her 'dead' husband and children

- the use of mentally ill people as 'entertainment' – the Duchess is forced to watch a masque of mad people

- secret love affairs of the aristocracy

- the control of women by their male relatives

- spying – Bosola is a secret agent in the Duchess' court

- 'unnatural' behaviour, threatening the stability of the country – Duke Ferdinand's insanity, in which he imagines himself a wolf and digs up dead bodies, overturns the hierarchy of nature: a man has descended to a beast.

The play expresses the familiar contemporary prejudice about the corruption of foreign, Catholic courts. But Jacobeans would hear echoes of their own criticisms of the English court of King James. When the Duke and Cardinal are described as 'like plumtrees that grow crooked over standing pools', many in Webster's audience would be reminded that James' court was also condemned for being like a stagnant pond. Right at the start of the play, Antonio's words might be a comment on what happened to England under James and his corrupt courtiers:

> A Prince's court
> Is like a common fountain, whence should flow
> Pure silver drops in general. But if it chance
> Some cursed example poison't near the head,
> Death and diseases through the whole land spread.

- Read the extract on pages 92–94. Why does the Duchess say 'I am Duchess of Malfi still'? Give your reaction to how she reacts to the prospect of death, and compare her death scene with that of Vittoria in *The White Devil* (pages 90–91).

The Revenger's Tragedy (c. 1605–1606)

Like all the Jacobean tragedies, the play stages the downfall of 'great men', whose pride and ambition end in death. *The Revenger's Tragedy* appealed to the Jacobeans' fascination with revenge, disguise and deceit, which pervade all aspects of its tangled plot.

Vindice is a malcontent. His beloved has been poisoned by the Duke. He swears revenge, and disguised, he becomes a servant of the Duke's son, Lussurioso. Vindice is horrified to find his mother is willing to let Lussurioso seduce his sister. The Duke's sons and stepsons plot against each other, and Vindice, pretending to help them, plans their downfall. He kills the Duke by tricking him into kissing a poisoned skull in the belief it is a woman. A masque is arranged to celebrate Lussurio becoming the new Duke. It becomes a bloodbath as Vindice and his brother Hippolito kill Lussurio and his nobles, the remaining sons kill each other, and sentence of execution is passed on Vindice and Hippolito.

The plot summary sounds like melodrama, but the play owes much to the tradition of morality plays (see page 20). Like those earlier plays, the characters' names signify their personal morality: Castiza, chastity; Lussurioso, lust; Vindice, vengeance; Gratiana, grace; Supervacuo, overfoolish; Ambitioso, ambitious. The Duke and his court embody the vices the Jacobeans attributed to foreign courts: lust, greed, pride and ambition. Spurio's heartless and self-seeking reaction to his father's death is typical:

> Old dad dead?
> I, one of his cast sins, will send the fates
> Most hearty commendation by his own son;
> I'll tug in the new stream, till strength be done

Modern audiences are often unsure whether or not they should laugh at this, and at other more bizarre moments. The uncertainty is increased by Middleton's use of the dramatic convention which allows characters to address the audience directly. For example, the play begins with Vindice commenting balefully and satirically on the court characters as they 'pass over the stage with torchlight', and many of his other speeches give similar opportunities to acknowledge the audience.

Almost every character is motivated by destructive passion, and is engaged in some villainy or deception. Many are like 'the biter bit': they become the victims of their own intrigues. The macabre and savage world of the play is created through its intense language and hyperbolic (greatly exaggerated) imagery. The descriptions of the corruption of the flesh in death echo the reminders of the consequences of sin that the Jacobeans heard each week in church.

The Revenger's Tragedy spoke directly to the Jacobeans' interest in revenge. English law prohibited revenge, seeing it as as a kind of 'wild justice'. But an earlier tradition of private revenge, linked to notions of personal honour, was still very much alive in the minds of the Jacobeans. They responded to Vindice's situation: he could not appeal to the law for justice, because the Duke (who was the law) had committed the crime. Personal revenge therefore seemed justified, but the Jacobeans, as Christians, found themselves caught between the contradictory teaching of the church. The Bible contained conflicting attitudes to revenge. The Old Testament called for 'life for life, eye for an eye, tooth for tooth, hand for hand, foot for foot, burning for burning, wound for wound, stripe for stripe' (Exodus 21.23–25). But in the New Testament, Jesus taught that enemies should be forgiven, and that victims should 'turn the other cheek'. Should a revenger take personal revenge or should he show mercy and forgiveness? The appeal of *The Revenger's Tragedy* was that, as in other tragedies of Webster and Middleton, the Jacobeans could enjoy vendettas and the unbridled pursuit of revenge, untroubled by all the doubts about its morality which beset them in real life.

▶ Read the extract on pages 94–95. How far do you agree with the accusation that it is more concerned with sadism than revenge. How would you stage it?

The Changeling (c. 1622)

The play is set in Alicante, Spain. Beatrice Joanna, daughter of the Governor, loves Alsemero, but her father intends her to marry Piracquo. Beatrice is loved by Deflores, her father's servant, whose facially deformed appearance she finds repulsive. She employs Deflores to murder Piracquo, but as a result falls into his power. As their sexual relationship develops, she becomes fascinated with Deflores. In a bizarre 'virginity test' Beatrice uses her maid, Diaphanta, to avoid Alsemero finding out the truth about her. Deflores kills Diaphanta, Alsemero discovers the truth at last, and Beatrice and Deflores kill themselves. The feeling that the tragedy moves inexorably to its climax is caught in Deflores' memorable cry 'Can you weep fate from its determined purpose?'

The sub-plot of *The Changeling* was written by William Rowley, who may also have contributed to the main plot (joint authorship was a common practice). It is set in an asylum of madmen. Antonio pretends to be mad, hoping his disguise will enable him to seduce Isabella, wife of the doctor who owns the asylum. She rejects his advances. The relationship of the sub-plot to the main plot has been much argued over. Both are concerned with illicit love that seeks to deceive husbands, and there is some agreement that just as Antonio is the Changeling (faking madness), so too is Beatrice. She is beautiful, and she talks much of 'honour', but she is corrupt, arranging murder to achieve her own desires.

The play clearly arises from its social and historical context, reflecting important concerns of the Jacobeans. Middleton includes references to contemporary events. When Diaphanta fears that Beatrice might subject her to a physical examination to determine if she is a virgin, she exclaims:

> She will not search me? Will she?
> Like the forewoman of a female jury?

Her words echo the divorce trial of the Countess of Essex (1613) in which she underwent such an examination by a panel of women. But beyond such 'local' references, the play reveals deeper concerns of the Jacobeans with money, sex, social status, and the belief that all Catholic states were corrupt. The play is not set in a royal court, but the Spanish society portrayed is the product of the same anti-Catholic, English prejudice and preconceptions that imagined Italian courts to be depraved. The alliance of Beatrice and Deflores in their murderous plots; the casual violence of the hacked-off finger; the deceptions and final suicides, all reinforced the Jacobeans' suspicions about foreigners. They would enjoy the exposure of hypocrisy in Deflores' rebuke to Beatrice: 'a woman dipt in blood, and talk of modesty?'

Another contemporary context is that of Jacobean attitudes to madness. Modern audiences often find the mad scenes uncomfortable to watch because they seem concerned to evoke laughter at the behaviour of mentally disturbed people. But Jacobeans were unembarrassed by lunatics. It was common practice to pay to watch them for amusement. Mentally disturbed people were the subjects of jokes, rather than of pity. Middleton exposes that for some people, lunatics were a profitable business. The Doctor who owns the asylum is invited to display his madmen at the celebrations for Beatrice's wedding. He tells his wife

> O wife, we must eat, wear clothes and live ...
> By madmen and by fools we both do thrive.

The play also displays Jacobean attitudes to women. Females were regarded as both chattels (possessions) and dangerous sexual objects. Beatrice is regarded by her father as something he owns and which he can dispose of however he wishes. Her desire for Alsemero, her arrangement for the murder of Piracquo, and her submission to Deflores' sexual demands, all reinforced Jacobean perceptions of the dangerous sensuality and unbridled desire of women. That preoccupation is further exposed by key words that echo through the play, all having meanings that can refer to sexual activity: 'service', 'will', 'act', 'deed'.

▶ Read the extract from *The Changeling* on pages 96–97. For much of the play, Beatrice seems to disregard the consequences of her deeds. What picture of her does Middleton present in this final scene?

▶ In the course of the play, Beatrice calls Deflores 'ill-faced', 'standing toadpool', 'Dog-face', and 'thou thing most loathed'. Yet his sexual conquest of her seems to make her develop affection for him. How would you stage their final moments together to show the nature of their relationship?

Women Beware Women (c. 1624)

Like other Jacobean tragedies, the play is based partly on an actual event and partly on fictional retellings of incest and lust in the Italian court of Tuscany. Leantio, a poor clerk, keeps his wife Bianca hidden. But she is seen at her window by the Duke of Florence. He wishes to seduce her, and Livia, a rich widow arranges the seduction. Bianca becomes the Duke's mistress. The Duke plans to kill Leantio. The murderer is Hippolito, who is enraged that his sister Livia has become Leantio's lover. Livia denounces Hippolito's lust for his own niece, and plans revenge. In a wedding masque in the final act, Bianca deliberately poisons herself, and other characters are killed with incense, poison, arrows, swords and trapdoors.

The play depicts the breakdown of personal morality in a permissive, acquisitive society. It can be interpreted as a searing comment on the corruption and lust of King James' court. Livia, who arranges the seduction of Bianca, is like the many pimps and procuresses who earned a living from the sexual licence of the Jacobean court. Women were bought and sold for sex, or for the 'marriage market' of the nobility. Extravagance and love of spectacle were other criticisms which find expression in the play, often in the imagery of jewellery, gluttony and treasure ('business' is used as a sexual pun).

The contempt for Leantio's low social class reflects James' courtiers' obsession with their high social station. Hippolito's desire for revenge on Leantio expresses a familiar feeling of the noblemen of the time: the thought that a female relative might have an affair with a social inferior was regarded with horror and the desire for vengeance (which usually took the form of hiring thugs to beat the man up). The play documents waste and sordid ruin, and in the context of later literature, it is significant that the game of chess, played while the Duke is seducing Bianca, gave T S Eliot the title of the second section of his poem *The Waste Land*.

The title of the play itself, warning of the treachery of women to each other, expresses a popular view of Jacobean court ladies' cynical disregard for others. Stories about how these women betrayed each other were common gossip. The

Earl of Worcester declared 'the plotting and malice amongst them is such that I think envy hath tied an invisible snake about most of their necks to sting one another to death'. Bianca's final words, just before she is killed by the poison she has drunk, could be the same criticism made through drama:

> Oh the deadly snares
> That women set for women, without pity
> Either to soul or honour! Learn by me
> To know your foes: in this belief I die,
> Like our own sex we have no enemy!
> Pride, greatness, honours, beauty, youth, ambition,
> You must all down together, there's no help for't.

▶ Use Bianca's seven lines above to analyse the Jacobean tragedy you know best. How accurately do they express what happens in the play? Also consider whether Bianca's words apply in any way to Shakespeare's tragedies.

Tragicomedy

A distinctive feature of all Shakespearean and Jacobean tragedy is that it is never 'pure' tragedy, relentlessly serious in tone. Humour keeps breaking into the tragic sequence of aspiration, suffering and death. All these tragedies incorporate **tragicomedy,** in which the mood switches from the sombre to the comic, characters and events are unexpectedly linked, and mocking wit or grotesque comedy breaks in. The playwrights knew that laughter, like death, is a great leveller. Lear is accompanied by a Fool, who comments derisively on his tragic plight, mocking his folly and lack of insight. The tragic hero's dignity (a quality much valued by the courtiers of Elizabeth and James) is put at risk by such characters.

The plays are full of punning and wordplay, and sardonic irony, as for example when Macbeth says to Banquo 'Fail not our feast'. Macbeth is making a little joke, known only to him. He has arranged Banquo's murder, so he knows that Banquo will certainly fail to attend the banquet. But Shakespeare gives Macbeth the words as an example of sardonic dramatic irony: what Macbeth does not know is that Banquo's Ghost will obey the command, and will appear to devastating effect.

Some Shakespearean characters invariably use humour, often ironically: Hamlet, Iago, Enobarbus. In Jacobean tragedies, the malcontents (see page 25) comment with sardonic humour on everything around them, and there are moments of bizarre or farcical comedy. In Shakespeare's tragedies, unexpected characters or events intrude into the serious action, disrupting the sombre mood at moments of high tragedy: the Porter in *Macbeth*, the clown who brings the asp to

Cleopatra, the Gravedigger in *Hamlet*, the musicians in *Romeo and Juliet*, the joking exchanges at the start of *Julius Caesar*, and the soldier who bursts in to the quarrel of Brutus and Cassius in *Julius Caesar*.

► Which tragic heroes have a sense of humour? Work through all the tragedies you know, identify the tragic characters in each, and say whether you think they have a sense of humour.

Assignments

1   Imagine you are the director of a Shakespearean or Jacobean tragedy of your choice. You wish to stage the play to bring out its contemporary relevance. Write the first talk you will give to your cast of actors telling them of your intentions, and how you hope to achieve your aims through set, costumes, characters and the language of the play.

2   Choose the tragedy you know best. Write the programme notes for a stage production explaining how the play relates to the time at which it was written.

3   Many people in Jacobean England believed that tragedy taught moral lessons. Do you agree that morality can be learned by reading or watching a tragedy? Select the tragedy you know best, suggest what moral lessons it might contain, then tell what you have learned from studying or seeing it. It might help you to know that some critics have dismissed Webster's plays as full of lurid horrors but empty of moral content, and written simply to make the audience's flesh creep.

4   Every tragedy discussed in this section uses the dramatic technique of 'juxtaposing scenes': making each scene comment in some way on the scene that precedes or follows it, contrasting with it, establishing a different atmosphere. Sometimes a single scene will contain very contrasting moods, for example beginning as comedy, but ending in tragedy. Choose one tragedy and work through it, identifying the contrasts between each scene and its following scene.

5   Select one main character and explain in detail how you would like to see him or her played on stage or in a film of the tragedy.

6 Revenge is the theme of many modern films, for example, *Return of the Jedi*, *Fatal Attraction*, *Die Hard*, *The Unforgiven*, *Dirty Harry*. In many films, an individual is denied revenge by the law, and so seeks it personally. Choose one film you know well and analyse it to show how it is both like and unlike Shakespearean and Jacobean tragedy.

7 What part does humour play in Shakespearean and Jacobean tragedy (episodes, characters, nature of the comedy, etc)? Use examples from several plays to illustrate your reply.

8 Do you think the mad scenes that occur in some of the tragedies can be called 'comic'? Select one, say whether or not you regard it as 'comic', and describe how you would stage it to greatest dramatic effect. Examples include Hamlet's 'antic disposition', Ophelia's bawdy songs, Lear's madness, the madmen in *The Changeling* and *The Duchess of Malfi*.

9 Why are Shakespeare's tragedies more frequently performed than those of Webster or Middleton? Write notes for a lecture you are to deliver on this question to a conference of school students who have only recently begun their study of the tragedies.

10 The Russian films of *Hamlet* and *King Lear* gave a significant presence to the ordinary people of Denmark and England. How would you film one other tragedy to show the presence and viewpoints of the common people?

11 Use the extracts on pages 72, 75, 85, 87, 90, 92 and 96 to identify the moods in which tragic characters face their death. What similarities and differences can you find? What do your findings tell you about the nature of 'tragic heroes'?

4 | Extracts from the tragedies

The extracts that follow have been chosen to illustrate key themes and points made elsewhere in the book, and to provide material which may be useful when working on the tasks and assignments in Parts 1, 2, 3, 5 and 6. The items are arranged chronologically (but see the comments on dates on pages 41 and 122).

Christopher Marlowe

From *Doctor Faustus* (c. 1589)

Doctor Faustus has sold his soul to the Devil in exchange for 24 years of power to do whatever he wishes. Now the 24 years are almost up. At midnight the Devil will come to claim Faustus and take him to hell. A clock strikes eleven.

FAUSTUS   Ah, Faustus,
Now hast thou but one bare hour to live,
And then thou must be damn'd perpetually.
Stand still, you ever-moving spheres of heaven,
That time may cease, and midnight never come.
Fair nature's eye, rise, rise again, and make
Perpetual day; or let this hour be but
A year, a month, a week, a natural day,
That Faustus may repent and save his soul.
O lente, lente, currite noctis equi!
The stars move still, time runs, the clock will strike,
The devil will come, and Faustus must be damn'd.
O, I'll leap up to my God! Who pulls me down?
See, see where Christ's blood streams in the firmament!
One drop would save my soul, half a drop. Ah, my Christ!
Rend not my heart for naming of my Christ!
Yet will I call on him. O, spare me, Lucifer!
Where is it now? 'Tis gone: and see where God
Stretcheth out his arm and bends his ireful brows.
Mountains and hills, come, come, and fall on me,
And hide me from the heavy wrath of God!
No, no:
Then will I run headlong into the earth.
Earth, gape! O, no, it will not harbour me.
You stars that reign'd at my nativity,
Whose influence hath allotted death and hell,
Now draw up Faustus like a foggy mist
Into the entrails of yon labouring cloud,

That when you vomit forth into the air,
My limbs may issue from your smoky mouths,
So that my soul may but ascend to heaven.
                [The clock strikes]
Ah, half the hour is pass'd, 'twill all be pass'd anon.
O God,
If thou wilt not have mercy on my soul,
Yet for Christ's sake, whose blood hath ransom'd me,
Impose some end to my incessant pain.
Let Faustus live in hell a thousand years,
A hundred thousand, and at last be sav'd.
O, no end is limited to damned souls.
Why wert thou not a creature wanting soul?
Or why is this immortal that thou hast?
Ah, Pythagoras' metempsychosis, were that true,
This soul should fly from me and I be chang'd
Unto some brutish beast.
All beasts are happy, for when they die
Their souls are soon dissolv'd in elements;
But mine must live still to be plagu'd in hell.
Curs'd be the parents that engender'd me!
No, Faustus, curse thyself, curse Lucifer
That hath depriv'd thee of the joys of heaven.
                [The clock striketh twelve]
O, it strikes, it strikes! Now, body, turn to air,
Or Lucifer will bear thee quick to hell!
                [Thunder and lightning]
O soul, be chang'd to little water drops,
And fall into the ocean, ne'er be found.
                [Enter Devils]
My God, my God! Look not so fierce on me!
Adders and serpents, let me breathe awhile!
Ugly hell, gape not! Come not, Lucifer!
I'll burn my books! Ah, Mephostophilis!
                [The Devils bear him away]
                        (Act 5 Scene 2: lines 133–190)

---

lente, lente, currite noctis equi O run
    slowly, slowly, horses of the night
Pythagoras' metempsychosis the belief in
    the transmigration of souls: that after
    death, the human soul migrated to an
    animal's body

Lucifer the Devil, Satan, the archangel who
    fell from heaven to hell
Mephostophilis agent of Lucifer

William Shakespeare

From *Titus Andronicus* (c. 1592)

Titus Andronicus' daughter Lavinia has been raped and mutilated by Chiron and Demetrius. They have cut off her hands and tongue. Now Titus has caught the two rapists and is about to take his revenge by killing them, cooking them, and serving them in a pie to their mother. He carries a knife, and Lavinia carries a basin.

TITUS   Come, come, Lavinia. Look thy foes are bound.
Sirs, stop their mouths. Let them not speak to me,
But let them hear what fearful words I utter.
O villains, Chiron and Demetrius!
Here stands the spring whom you have stained with mud,
This goodly summer with your winter mixed.
You killed her husband, and for that vile fault
Two of her brothers were condemned to death,
My hand cut off and made a merry jest,
Both her sweet hands, her tongue, and that more dear
Than hands or tongue, her spotless chastity,
Inhuman traitors, you constrained and forced.
What should you say if I should let you speak?
Villains, for shame. You could not beg for grace.
Hark, wretches, how I mean to martyr you.
This one hand yet is left to cut your throats,
Whiles that Lavinia 'tween her stumps doth hold
The basin that receives your guilty blood.
You know your mother means to feast with me,
And calls herself Revenge, and thinks me mad.
Hark, villains, I will grind your bones to dust,
And with your blood and it I'll make a paste,
And of the paste a coffin I will rear,
And make two pasties of your shameful heads,
And bid that strumpet, your unhallowed dam,
Like to the earth swallow her own increase.
This is the banquet I have bid her to,
And this the banquet she will surfeit on;
For worse than Philomel you used my daughter,
And worse than Procne I will be revenged.
And now, prepare your throats. Lavinia, come,
Receive the blood, and when that they are dead
Let me go grind their bones to powder small,
And with this hateful liquor temper it,
And in that paste let their vile heads be baked.

Come, come, be every one officious
To make this banquet, which I wish may prove
More stern and bloody than the Centaurs' feast.
        [He cuts their throats]
So, now bring them in, for I'll play the cook
And see them ready 'gainst their mother comes.

(Act 5 Scene 2: lines 166–205)

---

unhallowed dam unholy mother
Philomel, Procne in Greek mythology
Philomel was raped and mutilated by
Tereus. In revenge, her mother Procne
cooked Tereus' son in a pie and served it
to Tereus.

Centaurs' feast in Greek mythology
centaurs were half man, half horse. A
bloody battle followed their feast.

William Shakespeare

From *Richard III* (c. 1592–1593)

Richard has murdered his way to the throne of England. But now he faces
overthrow by the army of Richmond It is the night before the battle of Bosworth,
which will decide Richard's fate. In their tents on either side of the stage, Richard
and Richmond are sleeping. They are visited by the ghosts of Richard's victims who
curse Richard and bless Richmond. Six ghosts have already appeared, now the
Ghost of Lord Hastings speaks.

GHOST *[to Richard]* Bloody and guilty, guiltily awake
        And in a bloody battle end thy days!
        Think on Lord Hastings; despair, and die!
        [To Richmond] Quiet untroubled soul, awake, awake!
        Arm, fight, and conquer, for fair England's sake!   *[Exit]*
        [Enter the GHOSTS of the two young Princes]
GHOSTS *[to Richard]* Dream on thy cousins smothered in the Tower.
        Let us be lead within thy bosom, Richard,
        And weigh thee down to ruin, shame, and death!
        Thy nephews' souls bid thee despair, and die!
        [To Richmond] Sleep, Richmond, sleep in peace and wake
            in joy,
        Good angels guard thee from the boar's annoy!
        Live, and beget a happy race of kings!
        Edward's unhappy sons do bid thee flourish.   *[Exeunt]*

[Enter the GHOST OF ANNE, Richard's wife]

GHOST *[to Richard]* Richard, thy wife, that wretched Anne thy wife,
        That never slept a quiet hour with thee,
        Now fills thy sleep with perturbations,
        Tomorrow in the battle think on me,
        And fall thy edgeless sword; depair, and die!
        [To Richmond] Thou quiet soul, sleep thou a quiet sleep.
        Dream of success and happy victory!
        Thy adversary's wife doth pray for thee.   *[Exit]*

[Enter the GHOST OF BUCKINGHAM]

GHOST *[to Richard]* The first was I that helped thee to the crown;
        The last was I that felt thy tyranny.
        O, in the battle think on Buckingham,
        And die in terror of thy guiltiness!
        Dream on, dream on, of bloody deeds and death.
        Fainting, despair; despairing, yield thy breath!
        [To Richmond] I died for hope ere I could lend thee aid,
        But cheer thy heart and be thou not dismayed;
        God and good angels fight on Richmond's side,
        And Richard fall in height of all his pride!   *[Exit]*

[Richard starts out of his dream]

RICHARD   Give me another horse! Bind up my wounds!
        Have mercy, Jesu! – Soft! I did but dream.
        O coward conscience, how dost thou afflict me!
        The lights burn blue. It is not dead midnight.
        Cold fearful drops stand on my trembling flesh.
        What do I fear? Myself? There's none else by.
        Richard loves Richard: that is, I am I.
        Is there a murderer here? No. Yes, I am.
        Then fly. What, from myself? Great reason why:
        Lest I revenge. Myself upon myself?
        Alack, I love myself. Wherefore? For any good
        That I myself have done unto myself?
        O no! Alas, I rather hate myself
        For hateful deeds committed by myself.
        I am a villain. Yet I lie, I am not.
        Fool, of thyself speak well, Fool, do not flatter.
        My conscience hath a thousand several tongues,
        And every tongue brings in a several tale,
        And every tale condemns me for a villain.
        Perjury, perjury, in the highest degree.
        Murder, stern murder, in the direst degree,
        All several sins, all used in each degree,

     SHAKESPEAREAN AND JACOBEAN TRAGEDY

Throng to the bar, crying all 'Guilty! Guilty!'
I shall despair. There is no creature loves me;
And if I die, no soul will pity me.
Nay, wherefore should they, since that I myself
Find in myself no pity to myself?
Methought the souls of all that I had murdered
Came to my tent, and every one did threat
Tomorrow's vengeance on the head of Richard.

(Act 5 Scene 3: lines 149–209)

---

boar's annoy Richard's attacks (Richard's
   emblem was a wild boar)
several different

bar courtroom of trial

William Shakespeare

From *Richard II* (c. 1594)

John of Gaunt, close to death, paints a magnificent picture of an ideal England, but bitterly regrets that corruption has now brought it to ruin.

This royal throne of kings, this sceptred isle,
This earth of majesty, this seat of Mars,
This other Eden, demi-paradise,
This fortress built by Nature for herself
Against infection and the hand of war,
This happy breed of men, this little world,
This precious stone set in the silver sea
Which serves it in the office of a wall
Or as a moat defensive to a house
Against the envy of less happier lands,
This blessèd plot, this earth, this realm, this England,
This nurse, this teeming womb of royal kings
Feared by their breed and famous by their birth,
Renownèd for their deeds as far from home
For Christian service and true chivalry
As is the sepulchre in stubborn Jewry
Of the world's ransom, blessèd Mary's son,
This land of such dear souls, this dear, dear land,
Dear for her reputation through the world,
Is now leased out, I die pronouncing it,

Like to a tenement or pelting farm.
England, bound in with the triumphant sea
Whose rocky shore beats back the envious siege
Of watery Neptune, is now bound in with shame,
With inky blots and rotten parchment bonds,
That England that was wont to conquer others
Hath made a shameful conquest of itself.

(Act 2 Scene 1: lines 40–66)

---

sceptred (a sceptre is a symbol of a king's authority)

Mars god of war

Eden perfect place (home of Adam and Eve in the Bible)

office function

their breed other monarchs

sepulchre in stubborn Jewry Christ's tomb in Jerusalem

world's ransom (Christ's death was the ransom that paid for humanity's sins)

leased out shamefully rented

tenement or pelting farm rented smallholding or worthless farm

inky blots ... bonds corrupt contracts

William Shakespeare

From *Romeo and Juliet* (c. 1595)

The feud of the Montagues and Capulets has separated Romeo and Juliet, and Juliet's father is determined she shall marry Paris tomorrow. Friar Lawrence has persuaded Juliet to agree to a desperate action which will reunite her with Romeo. Juliet must drink a potion which will make her seem as though dead. When she is placed in the Capulet tomb, Romeo and the Friar will come to rescue her. In her bedroom, the night before her planned marriage, Juliet expresses her fears.

JULIET   My dismal scene I needs must act alone.
            Come, vial
            What if this mixture do not work at all?
            Shall I be married then tomorrow morning?
            No, no, this shall forbid it; lie thou there.
                [Lays down dagger]
            What if it be a poison which the Friar
            Subtly hath ministered to have me dead,
            Lest in this marriage he should be dishonoured,
            Because he married me before to Romeo?

I fear it is, and yet methinks it should not,
For he hath still been tried a holy man.
How if, when I am laid into the tomb,
I wake before the time that Romeo
Come to redeem me? There's a fearful point!
Shall I not then be stifled in the vault,
To whose foul mouth no healthsome air breathes in,
And there die strangled ere my Romeo comes?
Or if I live, is it not very like
The horrible conceit of death and night,
Together with the terror of the place –
As in a vault, an ancient receptacle,
Where for this many hundred years the bones
Of all my buried ancestors are packed,
Where bloody Tybalt, yet but green in earth,
Lies fest'ring in his shroud, where, as they say,
At some hours in the night spirits resort –
Alack, alack, is it not like that I,
So early waking – what with loathsome smells,
And shrieks like mandrakes' torn out of the earth,
That living mortals hearing then run mad –
O, if I wake, shall I not be distraught,
Environèd with all these hideous fears,
And madly play with my forefathers' joints
And pluck the mangled Tybalt from his shroud,
And in this rage, with some great kinsman's bone,
As with a club, dash out my desp'rate brains?
O look! methinks I see my cousin's ghost
Seeking out Romeo that did spit his body
Upon a rapier's point. Stay, Tybalt, stay!
Romeo, Romeo, Romeo! Here's drink – I drink to thee.

(Act 4 Scene 3: lines 19–58)

---

vial small bottle
conceit imagining
mandrakes plants that were believed
to shriek as they were pulled up

Environèd surrounded
spit skewer, pierce

William Shakespeare

From *Hamlet* (c. 1601)

HAMLET   To be, or not to be, that is the question –
Whether 'tis nobler in the mind to suffer
The slings and arrows of outrageous fortune,
Or to take arms against a sea of troubles,
And by opposing end them. To die, to sleep –
No more; and by a sleep to say we end
The heart-ache and the thousand natural shocks
That flesh is heir to – 'tis a consummation
Devoutly to be wished. To die, to sleep –
To sleep, perchance to dream. Ay, there's the rub,
For in that sleep of death what dreams may come,
When we have shuffled off this mortal coil,
Must give us pause. There's the respect
That makes calamity of so long life,
For who would bear the whips and scorns of time,
Th'oppressor's wrong, the proud man's contumely,
The pangs of disprized love, the law's delay,
The insolence of office, and the spurns
That patient merit of th'unworthy takes,
When he himself might his quietus make
With a bare bodkin? Who would fardels bear,
To grunt and sweat under a weary life,
But that the dread of something after death,
The undiscovered country from whose bourn
No traveller returns, puzzles the will,
And makes us rather bear those ills we have
Than fly to others that we know not of?
Thus conscience does make cowards of us all,
And thus the native hue of resolution
Is sicklied o'er with the pale cast of thought,
And enterprises of great pitch and moment
With this regard their currents turn awry
And lose the name of action. Soft you now,
The fair Ophelia. – Nymph, in thy orisons
Be all my sins remembered.

(Act 3 Scene 1: lines 56–90)

SHAKESPEAREAN AND JACOBEAN TRAGEDY

consummation ending
rub obstacle
shuffled off this mortal coil died (shaken
  off the confusions of human life)
contumely humiliating insults
quietus release
bodkin dagger

fardels burden
sicklied o'er unhealthily covered
pitch and moment importance
orisons prayers

William Shakespeare

From *Othello* (c. 1604)

Iago, pretending to be honest, has fanned Othello's jealousy into raging passion.
Othello now believes that his wife Desdemona has been unfaithful to him with his
lieutenant, Cassio. Iago invents his final lie to increase Othello's fury and desire for
murderous revenge.

IAGO	Nay, yet be wise; yet we see nothing done,
	She may be honest yet. Tell me but this:
	Have you not sometimes seen a handkerchief
	Spotted with strawberries in your wife's hand?
OTHELLO	I gave her such a one; 'twas my first gift.
IAGO	I know not that; but such a handkerchief –
	I am sure it was your wife's – did I today
	See Cassio wipe his beard with.
OTHELLO	If it be that –
IAGO	If it be that, or any that was hers,
	It speaks against her with the other proofs.
OTHELLO	O that the slave had forty thousand lives!
	One is too poor, too weak, for my revenge.
	Now do I see 'tis true. Look here, Iago,
	All my fond love thus do I blow to heaven;
	'Tis gone.
	Arise, black vengeance, from thy hollow cell!
	Yield up, O love, thy crown and hearted throne
	To tyrannous hate! Swell, bosom, with thy fraught,
	For 'tis of aspics' tongues. *[He kneels]*
IAGO	Yet be content.
OTHELLO	O, blood, blood, blood!
IAGO	Patience, I say; your mind perhaps may change.

OTHELLO	Never, Iago. Like to the Pontic Sea,
	Whose icy current and compulsive course
	Ne'er feels retiring ebb but keeps due on
	To the Propontic and the Hellespont,
	Even so my bloody thoughts with violent pace
	Shall ne'er look back, ne'er ebb to humble love,
	Till that a capable and wide revenge
	Swallow them up. Now by yond marble heaven,
	In the due reverence of a sacred vow
	I here engage my words.
IAGO	Do not rise yet. *[He kneels]*
	Witness you ever-burning lights above,
	You elements that clip us round about,
	Witness that here Iago doth give up
	The execution of his wit, hands, heart,
	To wronged Othello's service. Let him command,
	And to obey shall be in me remorse,
	What bloody business ever. *[They rise]*
OTHELLO	I greet thy love,
	Not with vain thanks, but with acceptance bounteous;
	And will upon the instant put thee to't.
	Within these three days let me hear thee say
	That Cassio's not alive.
IAGO	My friend is dead;
	'Tis done at your request. But let her live.
OTHELLO	Damn her, lewd minx! O, damn her, damn her!
	Come, go with me apart. I will withdraw
	To furnish me with some swift means of death
	For the fair devil. Now art thou my lieutenant.
IAGO	I am your own for ever.

(Act 3 Scene 3: lines 433–480)

---

fraught cargo, burden
aspic venomous snake
Pontic, Propontic, Hellespont
  all adjacent to Turkey: Black Sea, Sea of
  Marmora, the Dardanelles

capable ample, full
clip embrace

William Shakespeare

From *King Lear* (c. 1605)

King Lear has banished his youngest daughter Cordelia and divided his kingdom
between his other daughters, Gonerill and Regan. But he still expects to be obeyed
in everything and is enraged when Gonerill dismisses 50 of his knights. Lear curses
Gonerill, saying Regan will treat him better, but both daughters join forces to take
away all his power.

LEAR	I prithee, daughter, do not make me mad.
	I will not trouble thee, my child. Farewell.
	We'll no more meet, no more see one another.
	But yet thou art my flesh, my blood, my daughter,
	Or rather a disease that's in my flesh,
	Which I must needs call mine. Thou art a boil,
	A plague-sore, or embossèd carbuncle
	In my corrupted blood. But I'll not chide thee;
	Let shame come when it wilt, I do not call it.
	I do not bid the thunder-bearer shoot,
	Nor tell tales of thee to high-judging Jove.
	Mend when thou canst, be better at thy leisure,
	I can be patient, I can stay with Regan,
	I and my hundred knights.
REGAN	Not altogether so.
	I looked not for you yet, nor am provided
	For your fit welcome. Give ear, sir, to my sister,
	For those that mingle reason with your passion
	Must be content to think you old, and so –
	But she knows what she does.
LEAR	Is this well spoken?
REGAN	I dare avouch it, sir. What, fifty followers?
	Is it not well? What should you need of more?
	Yea, or so many, sith that both charge and danger
	Speak 'gainst so great a number? How in one house
	Should many people under two commands
	Hold amity? 'Tis hard, almost impossible.
GONERILL	Why might not you, my lord, receive attendance
	From those that she calls servants, or from mine?
REGAN	Why not, my Lord? If then they chanced to slack ye,
	We could control them. If you will come to me
	(For now I spy a danger) I entreat you
	To bring but five and twenty; to no more

	Will I give place or notice.
LEAR	I gave you all.
REGAN	And in good time you gave it.
LEAR	Made you my guardians, my depositaries,
	But kept a reservation to be followed
	With such a number. What, must I come to you
	With five and twenty? Regan, said you so?
REGAN	And speak't again, my lord. No more with me.
LEAR	Those wicked creatures yet do look well-favoured
	When others are more wicked. Not being the worst
	Stands in some rank of praise. *[To Gonerill]* I'll go with thee;
	Thy fifty yet doth double five and twenty,
	And thou art twice her love.
GONERILL	Hear me, my Lord:
	What need you five and twenty? ten? or five?
	To follow in a house where twice so many
	Have a command to tend you?
REGAN	What need one?
LEAR	O reason not the need! Our basest beggars
	Are in the poorest thing superfluous.
	Allow not nature more than nature needs,
	Man's life is cheap as beast's. Thou art a lady;
	If only to go warm were gorgeous,
	Why nature needs not what thou gorgeous wear'st,
	Which scarcely keeps thee warm. But for true need –
	You heavens give me patience, patience I need.
	You see me here, you gods, a poor old man,
	As full of grief as age, wretched in both;
	If it be you that stirs these daughters' hearts
	Against their father, fool me not so much
	To bear it tamely. Touch me with noble anger,
	And let not women's weapons, water drops,
	Stain my man's cheeks. No, you unnatural hags,
	I will have such revenges on you both
	That all the world shall – I will do such things –
	What they are, yet I know not, but they shall be
	The terrors of the earth! You think I'll weep;
	No, I'll not weep,
	[Storm and tempest]
	I have full cause of weeping, but this heart
	Shall break into a hundred thousand flaws
	Or ere I'll weep. O fool, I shall go mad.

(Act 2 Scene 4: lines 211–279)

William Shakespeare

From *Macbeth* (c. 1606)

Macbeth has murdered Duncan and become King of Scotland. But his tyrannical rule is challenged, and now his enemies are closing in on him in his castle at Dunsinane.

MACBETH	Hang out our banners on the outward walls;
	The cry is still, 'They come'. Our castle's strength
	Will laugh a siege to scorn; here let them lie
	Till famine and the ague eat them up.
	Were they not forced with those that should be ours,
	We might have met them dareful, beard to beard,
	And beat them backward home.
	[A cry within of women]
	What is that noise?
SEYTON	It is the cry of women, my good lord.
MACBETH	I have almost forgot the taste of fears;
	The time has been, my senses would have cooled
	To hear a night-shriek and my fell of hair
	Would at a dismal treatise rouse and stir
	As life were in't. I have supped full with horrors;
	Direness familiar to my slaughterous thoughts
	Cannot once start me. Wherefore was that cry?
SEYTON	The queen, my lord, is dead.
MACBETH	She should have died hereafter;
	There would have been a time for such a word.
	Tomorrow, and tomorrow, and tomorrow
	Creeps in this petty pace from day to day
	To the last syllable of recorded time;
	And all our yesterdays have lighted fools

The way to dusty death. Out, out, brief candle,
Life's but a walking shadow, a poor player
That struts and frets his hour upon the stage
And then is heard no more. It is a tale
Told by an idiot, full of sound and fury
Signifying nothing.
[Enter a MESSENGER]
Thou com'st to use thy tongue: thy story quickly.

MESSENGER   Gracious my lord,
I should report that which I say I saw,
But know not how to do't.

MACBETH   Well, say sir.

MESSENGER   As I did stand my watch upon the hill
I looked toward Birnam and anon methought
The wood began to move.

MACBETH   Liar and slave!

MESSENGER   Let me endure your wrath if't be not so;
Within this three mile may you see it coming.
I say, a moving grove.

MACBETH   If thou speak'st false,
Upon the next tree shall thou hang alive
Till famine cling thee; if thy speech be sooth,
I care not if thou dost for me as much.
I pull in resolution and begin
To doubt th'equivocation of the fiend
That lies like truth. 'Fear not, till Birnam Wood
Do come to Dunsinane', and now a wood
Comes toward Dunsinane. Arm, arm, and out!
If this which he avouches does appear,
There is nor flying hence nor tarrying here.
I 'gin to be aweary of the sun
And wish th'estate o'th'world were now undone.
Ring the alarum bell! Blow wind, come wrack;
At least we'll die with harness on our back.   *[Exeunt]*

(Act 5 Scene 5: lines 1–51)

---

forced reinforced

my fell of hair every hair on my body

treatise story

start frighten

watch guard duty

cling wither

sooth true

pull in resolution lose confidence

equivocation double-talk

avouches says is true

tarrying waiting

harness armour

SHAKESPEAREAN AND JACOBEAN TRAGEDY

William Shakespeare

From *Antony and Cleopatra* (c. 1606)

Antony has committed suicide, and Cleopatra has determined she will not be taken as a prisoner to Rome. She has been brought poisonous snakes, and now she prepares to die like a great queen, dressed in her finest robes by her serving women, Charmian and Iras.

CLEOPATRA   Give me my robe. Put on my crown. I have
            Immortal longings in me. Now no more
            The juice of Egypt's grape shall moist this lip.
                     [The women dress her]
            Yare, yare, good Iras; quick. Methinks I hear
            Antony call. I see him rouse himself
            To praise my noble act. I hear him mock
            The luck of Caesar, which the gods give men
            To excuse their after wrath. Husband, I come!
            Now to that name my courage prove my title!
            I am fire and air; my other elements
            I give to baser life. So, have you done?
            Come, then, and take the last warmth of my lips.
            Farewell, kind Charmian. Iras, long farewell.
                     [She kisses them. Iras falls and dies]
            Have I the aspic in my lips? Dost fall?
            If thou and nature can so gently part,
            The stroke of death is as a lover's pinch,
            Which hurts, and is desired. Dost thou lie still?
            If thus thou vanishest, thou tell'st the world
            It is not worth leave-taking.
CHARMIAN   Dissolve, thick cloud, and rain, that I may say
            The gods themselves do weep!
CLEOPATRA   This proves me base.
            If she first meet the curlèd Antony,
            He'll make demand of her, and spend that kiss
            Which is my heaven to have. Come, thou mortal wretch,
                     [She applies an asp]
            With thy sharp teeth this knot intrinsicate
            Of life at once untie. Poor venomous fool,
            Be angry, and dispatch. O, couldst thou speak,
            That I might hear thee call great Caesar ass
            Unpolicied!
CHARMIAN   O eastern star!

CLEOPATRA	Peace, peace!
	Dost thou not see my baby at my breast,
	That sucks the nurse asleep?
CHARMIAN	O, break, O, break!
CLEOPATRA	As sweet as balm, as soft as air, as gentle –
	O Antony! – Nay, I will take thee too.
	[She applies another asp]
	What should I stay – *[Dies]*
CHARMIAN	In this wild world? So, fare thee well.
	Now boast thee, Death, in thy possession lies
	A lass unparalleled. Downy windows, close;
	And golden Phoebus never be beheld
	Of eyes again so royal! Your crown's awry;
	I'll mend it, and then play –
	[Enter the GUARD rustling in]
1 GUARD	Where's the queen?
CHARMIAN	Speak softly. Wake her not.
1 GUARD	Caesar hath sent –
CHARMIAN	Too slow a messenger.
	[She applies an asp]
	O, come apace, dispatch! I partly feel thee.
1 GUARD	Approach, ho! All's not well. Caesar's beguiled.
2 GUARD	There's Dolabella sent from Caesar. Call him.
	[Exit a Guardsman]
1 GUARD	What work is here, Charmian? Is this well done?
CHARMIAN	It is well done, and fitting for a princess
	Descended of so many royal kings.
	Ah, soldier! *[Charmian dies]*
	(Act 5 Scene 2: lines 274–322)

Yare quickly
aspic poison of the asp
curlèd curly headed
intrinsicate intricate, mysterious

Unpolicied outmanoeuvred
Phoebus the sun god
rustling clattering

William Shakespeare

From *Timon of Athens* (c. 1608)

Timon had entertained all his friends with overwhelming generosity. But when his money ran out, they refused to help him. Their ingratitude has turned him into a misanthrope (a hater of humankind), and he now reviles Athens, wishing misery and suffering on all within the city.

TIMON   Let me look back upon thee. O thou wall
That girdles in those wolves, dive in the earth,
And fence not Athens. Matrons, turn incontinent.
Obedience fail in children. Slaves and fools
Pluck the grave wrinkled Senate from the bench,
And minister in their steads. To general filths
Convert o'th'instant green virginity.
Do't in your parents' eyes. Bankrupts, hold fast;
Rather than render back, out with your knives
And cut your trusters' throats. Bound servants, steal.
Large-handed robbers your grave masters are,
And pill by law. Maid, to thy master's bed;
Thy mistress is o'th'brothel. Son of sixteen,
Pluck the lined crutch from thy old limping sire,
With it beat out his brains. Piety and fear,
Religion to the gods, peace, justice, truth,
Domestic awe, night-rest, and neighbourhood,
Instruction, manners, mysteries, and trades,
Degrees, observances, customs, and laws,
Decline to your confounding contraries
And let confusion live. Plagues incident to men,
Your potent and infectious fevers heap
On Athens, ripe for stroke. Thou cold sciatica,
Cripple our senators, that their limbs may halt
As lamely as their manners. Lust and liberty
Creep in the minds and marrows of our youth,
That 'gainst the stream of virtue they may strive,
And drown themselves in riot. Itches, blains,
Sow all th'Athenian bosoms, and their crop
Be general leprosy. Breath infect breath,
That their society, as their friendship, may
Be merely poison. Nothing I'll bear from thee
But nakedness, thou detestable town.
Take thou that too, with multiplying bans.

Timon will to the woods, where he shall find
The unkindest beast more kinder than mankind.
The gods confound – hear me, you good gods all –
Th'Athenians both within and out that wall.
And grant, as Timon grows, his hate may grow
To the whole race of mankind, high and low.
Amen

(Act 4 Scene 1: lines 1–41)

---

incontinent lustful	**Domestic awe** family harmony
minister rule	**mysteries** crafts
pill steal	**Degrees** social rankings
sire father	**observances** duties

John Webster

From *The White Devil* (c. 1612)

Vittoria and her brother Flamineo face death together at the hands of agents of Vittoria's enemy. Vittoria's husband and her maid Zanche have been killed, and now the murderers' swords give Vittoria and Flamineo their death blows.

VITTORIA   'Twas a manly blow.
The next thou giv'st, murder some sucking infant,
And then thou wilt be famous.

FLAMINEO   O what blade is't?
A toledo, or an English fox?
I ever thought a cutler should distinguish
The cause of my death, rather than a doctor.
Search my wound deeper: tent it with the steel
That made it.

VITTORIA   O my greatest sin lay in my blood.
Now my blood pays for't.

FLAMINEO   Th'art a noble sister,
I love thee now; if woman do breed man
She ought to teach him manhood. Fare thee well.
Know many glorious women that are fam'd
For masculine virtue, have been vicious,
Only a happier silence did betide them.
She hath no faults, who hath the art to hide them.

VITTORIA   My soul, like to a ship in a black storm,

	Is driven I know not whither.
FLAMINEO	Then cast anchor.
	Prosperity doth bewitch men seeming clear,
	But seas do laugh, show white, when rocks are near.
	We cease to grieve, cease to be Fortune's slaves,
	Nay cease to die by dying. *[to ZANCHE]* Art thou gone?
	[to VITTORIA] And thou so near the bottom? False report
	Which says that women vie with the nine Muses
	For nine tough durable lives. I do not look
	Who went before, nor who shall follow me:
	No, at myself I will begin and end.
	While we look up to heaven we confound
	Knowledge with knowledge. O I am in a mist.
VITTORIA	O happy they that never saw the court,
	Nor ever knew great men but by report. *[Dies]*
FLAMINEO	I recover like a spent taper, for a flash
	And instantly go out.
	Let all that belong to great men remember th'old wives'
	tradition, to be like the lions i'th' Tower on Candlemas day,
	to mourn if the sun shine, for fear of the pitiful remainder
	of winter to come.
	'Tis well yet there's some goodness in my death,
	My life was a black charnel. I have caught
	An everlasting cold. I have lost my voice
	Most irrevocably. Farewell glorious villains,
	This busy trade of life appears most vain,
	Since rest breeds rest, where all seek pain by pain.
	Let no harsh flattering bells resound my knell,
	Strike thunder, and strike loud to my farewell. *[Dies]*

(Act 5 Scene 6: lines 230–274)

---

toledo high quality Spanish sword
cutler swordmaker
tent probe
betide cover
nine Muses immortal goddesses

spent taper burnt-out firelighter
Candlemas February 2nd (when candles are blessed)
charnel house of bones
knell funeral bell

John Webster

From *The Duchess of Malfi* (c. 1614)

On her brothers' orders, the Duchess of Malfi has been cruelly tormented with madmen and images of her dead husband and children. Now Bosola, a malcontent in the service of her brothers, tells the Duchess of her imminent death. Her faithful serving woman, Cariola, tries to protect her.

BOSOLA   I am the common bellman,
That usually is sent to condemn'd persons,
The night before they suffer.

DUCHESS   Even now thou said'st
Thou wast a tomb-maker?

BOSOLA   'Twas to bring you
By degrees to mortification. Listen:
[He rings the bell]
Hark, now every thing is still,
The screech-owl and the whistler shrill
Call upon our Dame, aloud,
And bid her quickly don her shroud.
Much you had of land and rent,
Your length in clay's now competent.
A long war disturb'd your mind,
Here your perfect peace is sign'd.
Of what is't fools make such vain keeping?
Sin their conception, their birth, weeping:
Their life, a general mist of error,
Their death, a hideous storm of terror.
Strew your hair with powders sweet:
Don clean linen, bathe your feet,
And, the foul fiend more to check,
A crucifix let bless your neck.
'Tis now full tide 'tween night and day,
End your groan, and come away.
[The Executioners approach]

CARIOLA   Hence villains, tyrants, murderers. Alas!
What will you do with my lady? Call for help.

DUCHESS   To whom, to our next neighbours? They are mad-folks.

BOSOLA   Remove that noise.
[Executioners seize Cariola, who struggles]

DUCHESS   Farewell Cariola,
In my last will I have not much to give;

	A many hungry guests have fed upon me,
	Thine will be a poor reversion.
CARIOLA	I will die with her.
DUCHESS	I pray thee look thou giv'st my little boy
	Some syrup for his cold, and let the girl
	Say her prayers, ere she sleep.

[Cariola is forced off]

DUCHESS	Now what you please, what death?
BOSOLA	Strangling: here are your executioners.
DUCHESS	I forgive them:
	The apoplexy, catarrh, or cough o'th'lungs
	Would do as much as they do.
BOSOLA	Doth not death fright you?
DUCHESS	Who would be afraid on't?
	Knowing to meet such excellent company
	In th'other world.
BOSOLA	Yet, methinks,
	The manner of your death should much afflict you,
	This cord should terrify you?
DUCHESS	Not a whit:
	What would it pleasure me, to have my throat cut
	With diamonds? or to be smothered
	With cassia? or to be shot to death, with pearls?
	I know death hath ten thousand several doors
	For men to take their exits: and 'tis found
	They go on such strange geometrical hinges,
	You may open them both ways: any way, for Heaven sake,
	So I were out of your whispering. Tell my brothers
	That I perceive death, now I am well awake,
	Best gift is, they can give, or I can take.
	I would fain put off my last woman's fault,
	I'll'd not be tedious to you.
EXECUTIONERS	We are ready.
DUCHESS	Dispose my breath how please you, but my body
	Bestow upon my women, will you?
EXECUTIONERS	Yes.
DUCHESS	Pull, and pull strongly, for your able strength
	Must pull down heaven upon me:
	Yet stay, heaven gates are not so highly arch'd
	As princes' palaces: they that enter there
	Must go upon their knees. Come violent death,
	Serve for mandragora to make me sleep;
	Go tell my brothers, when I am laid out,

They then may feed in quiet.

[They strangle her]

(Act 4 Scene 2: lines 171–233)

---

bellman see page 35
reversion legacy

cassia cinnamon
mandragora narcotic plant

Thomas Middleton

From *The Revenger's Tragedy* (c. 1605–1606)

Vindice seeks revenge upon the Duke for the murder of his beloved lady, Gloriana. He has entered the service of the Duke in disguise as Piato. He prepares Gloriana's poisoned skull and intends the Duke to kiss it, thinking it is a beautiful woman. With his brother Hippolito, he awaits the Duke's entrance.

VINDICE This very skull,
Whose mistress the Duke poisoned, with this drug
The mortal curse of the earth, shall be reveng'd
In the like strain, and kiss his lips to death;
As much as the dumb thing can, he shall feel:
What fails in poison, we'll supply in steel.

HIPPOLITO Brother I do applaud thy constant vengeance,
The quaintness of thy malice above thought.
[Vindice puts poison on the skull's lips]

VINDICE So 'tis laid on: now come and welcome, Duke,
I have her for thee. I protest brother:
Methinks she makes almost as fair a sign
As some old gentleman in a periwig.
[Puts a mask on the skull]
Hide thy face now for shame, thou hadst need have a mask now,
'Tis vain when beauty flows, but when it fleets
This would become graves better than the streets.

HIPPOLITO You have my voice in that. Hark, the Duke's come.

VINDICE Peace, let's observe what company he brings,
And how he does absent 'em, for you know
He'll wish all private. Brother, fall you back a little
With the bony lady.

HIPPOLITO That I will

VINDICE	So, so, –
	Now nine years' vengeance crowd into a minute!
	[Enter DUKE and GENTLEMEN]
DUKE	You shall have leave to leave us, with this charge,
	Upon your lives, if we be miss'd by th'Duchess
	Or any of the nobles, to give out,
	We're privately rid forth!
VINDICE	*[Aside]* Oh happiness!
DUKE	With some few honourable gentlemen you may say,
	You may name those that are away from court.
GENTLEMEN	Your will and pleasure shall be done my Lord. *[Exeunt]*
VINDICE	*[Aside]* Privately rid forth!
	He strives to make sure work on't – Your good Grace?
DUKE	Piato, well done. Hast brought her? What lady is't?
VINDICE	Faith my Lord a country lady, a little bashful at first as most
	of them are, but after the first kiss my Lord the worst is
	past with them; your Grace knows now what you have to
	do; sh'as somewhat a grave look with her – but –
DUKE	I love that best; conduct her.
VINDICE	*[Aside]* Have at all.
DUKE	In gravest looks the greatest faults seem less,
	Give me that sin that's rob'd in holiness.
VINDICE	*[Aside]* Back with the torch; brother raise the perfumes.
DUKE	How sweet can a duke breathe! Age has no fault,
	Pleasure should meet in a perfumed mist.
	Lady, sweetly encount'red;
	I came from court, I must be bold with you.
	[Kisses skull]
	Oh, what's this? oh!
VINDICE	Royal villain, white devil!
DUKE	Oh!
VINDICE	Brother –
	Place the torch here, that his affrighted eye-balls
	May start into those hollows, Duke, dost know
	Yon dreadful vizard? View it well, 'tis the skull
	Of Gloriana, whom thou poisonedst last.
DUKE	Oh, 't'as poisoned me.
VINDICE	Didst not know that till now?
DUKE	What are you two?
VINDICE	Villains all three! – The very ragged bone
	Has been sufficiently reveng'd.
DUKE	Oh, Hippolito! call treason.
HIPPOLITO	Yes my good Lord, treason, treason, treason.

	[Stamping on him]
DUKE	Then I'm betray'd
VINDICE	Alas poor lecher in the hands of knaves.
	A slavish duke is baser than his slaves.
DUKE	My teeth are eaten out.
VINDICE	Hadst any left?
HIPPOLITO	I think but few.
VINDICE	Then those that did eat are eaten.
DUKE	O my tongue!
VINDICE	Your tongue? 'twill teach you to kiss closer,
	Not like a flobbering Dutchman – you have eyes still:
	Look monster, what a lady hast thou made me,
	My once betrothed wife.
DUKE	Is it thou, villain?
	Nay then –
VINDICE	'Tis I, 'tis Vindice, 'tis I.

(Act 3 Scene 5: lines 101–168)

---

periwig wig

vizard mask, face

lecher disgusting lustful man

Thomas Middleton

From *The Changeling* (c. 1622)

Beatrice Joanna had employed Deflores (whom she loathed) to murder an unwanted suitor so that she could marry Alsemero. But Deflores used their criminal relationship to enjoy a sexual relationship with Beatrice, and she has developed an affection for him. Beatrice paid her maid Diaphanta to sleep with Alsemero, so that her own loss of virginity would not be revealed. But all is now discovered and Deflores stabs Beatrice and carries her, wounded, to her husband and her father, Vermandero.

DEFLORES	Here we are; if you have any more
	To say to us, speak quickly, I shall not
	Give you the hearing else, I am so stout yet,
	And so I think that broken rib of mankind.
VERMANDERO	An host of enemies ent'red my citadel
	Could not amaze like this – Joanna, Beatrice, Joanna!
BEATRICE	O come not near me sir. I shall defile you;

	I am that of your blood was taken from you
	For your better health, look no more upon't,
	But cast it to the ground regardlessly,
	Let the common sewer take it from distinction.
	Beneath the stars, upon yon meteor
	Ever hung my fate, 'mongst things corruptible,
	I ne'er could pluck it from him, my loathing
	Was prophet to the rest, but ne'er believed;
	Mine honour fell with him, and now my life.
	Alsemero, I am a stranger to your bed,
	Your bed was coz'ned on the nuptial night,
	For which your false bride died.
ALSEMERO	Diaphanta!
DEFLORES	Yes, and the while I coupled with your mate
	At barley-brake; now we are left in hell.
VERMANDERO	We are all there, it circumscribes here.
DEFLORES	I lov'd this woman in spite of her heart,
	Her love I earn'd out of Piracquo's murder.
TOMAZO	Ha, my brother's murtherer.
DEFLORES	Yes, and her honour's prize
	Was my reward, I thank life for nothing
	But that pleasure, it was so sweet to me
	That I have drunk up all, left none behind
	For any man to pledge me.
VERMANDERO	Horrid villain!
	Keep life in him for further tortures.
DEFLORES	No,
	I can prevent you, here's my penknife still,
	It is but one thread more, *[stabs himself]* – and now 'tis cut.
	Make haste Joanna, by that token to thee.
	Canst not forget, so lately put in mind,
	I would not go to leave thee far behind. *[Dies]*
BEATRICE	Forgive me Alsemero, all forgive,
	'Tis time to die, when 'tis a shame to live. *[Dies]*

(Act 5 Scene 3: lines 145–181)

coz'ned cheated   circumscribes surrounds

coupled had sex with

barley-brake a children's game in which a
  couple are caught

5 | Critical approaches

- How have critical approaches to Shakespearean and Jacobean tragedy changed?

- How were Shakespearean and Jacobean tragedies traditionally discussed by critics?

- What are the main types of criticism today?

In the last quarter of the 20th century, critical approaches to Shakespearean and Jacobean drama were radically transformed. Tragedy in particular became a key battleground for competing interpretations. New critical approaches argued that traditional interpretations of tragedy were detached from the real world, and were elitist, sexist, unpolitical and individualist. Why? Because traditional criticism divorced literary, dramatic and aesthetic matters from their social context.

The new critical approaches (which can be called 'modern criticism') claim that the study of tragedy should focus on the historical and social factors which influenced Shakespeare and the Jacobean playwrights. They also examine how the political and cultural factors in each different age influence how the plays have been read, staged and interpreted (in critical language this is expressed as 'history determining the production and reception of the plays'). This book is therefore an example of modern approaches which seek to place the tragedies of Shakespeare, Webster and Middleton in the context of their times.

The summary opposite identifies the major differences between traditional and modern criticism.

▶ Use the table opposite with the tragedy you know best. Consider each of the nine points in turn and suggest how a 'traditional' and a 'modern' (or 'radical') critic might respond to the play for each item. For example, under point 2 a traditional critic might argue that the tragedy is caused by a flaw in Hamlet's character; a radical critic might claim that the tragedy is caused by Denmark's corrupt society.

Traditional critical approaches

There have been many notable critics of Shakespearean and Jacobean tragedy, for example Samuel Johnson in the 18th century and Samuel Taylor Coleridge in the 19th. But for students beginning serious study of the tragedies, the immediately significant criticism dates from the 20th century. Such criticism embodies many of the insights and assumptions of earlier critics such as Johnson and Coleridge.

A comparison of the major differences between traditional and modern criticism of Shakespearean and Jacobean tragedy

Traditional criticism	Modern criticism
1 Claims to be objective and free from bias.	1 Expresses its commitment (for example, to feminism, or equality, or political change).
2 Sees tragedy as being centrally about an individual who suffers and dies because of some chance happening or personal character flaw.	2 Sees tragedy as about political, social and economic factors; stresses how tragedy serves the interests of dominant groups, e.g. rich and powerful males.
3 Stresses the supernatural or mysterious and inexplicable causes of tragedy, and ignores its social determinants.	3 Plays down the supernatural and mysterious, and offers social explanations of tragedy.
4 Sees tragedy as inevitable and inescapable, to be endured, not resisted.	4 Sees tragedy as avoidable, and to be challenged and resisted.
5 Sees, at the end of a tragedy, hope and harmony after suffering and death.	5 Sees no necessary reconciliatory or 'hopeful' ending to a tragedy.
6 Interprets the tragedies as having coherence and unity.	6 Sees tragedy as full of contradictions and disunity.
7 Rejects 'theory' in understanding drama.	7 Insists that 'theory' is essential to produce valid readings.
8 Produces readings which support existing social structures.	8 Produces readings which are subversive of existing social structures.
9 Assumes that 'straightforward' or 'commonsense' interpretations of tragedy are possible and preferable.	9 Argues that all interpretations are influenced by preconceptions, and, that 'straightforward' or 'commonsense' readings are suspect.

A C Bradley: the study of character

Almost 100 years ago, the critic A C Bradley delivered a number of lectures at Oxford University which were published in 1904 as *Shakespearean Tragedy*. The book has never been out of print, and Bradley's approach has been hugely influential on the study of Shakespearean and Jacobean tragedies. Bradley considered only four plays as 'pure tragedies': *Hamlet, Othello, King Lear* and *Macbeth*. Although he has been much criticised, Bradley's key assumptions still dominate how these tragedies are taught in schools. His approach can be characterised in two words: **'character criticism'**.

Bradley talked of the characters in the tragedies as if they were real human beings existing in worlds recognisable to modern readers. For him, each character experienced familiar human emotions and thoughts. Bradley sought out the unique desires and motives which gave each character their particular personality, and which evoked feelings of admiration or disapproval in the audience. He argued that the conflict in the plays is primarily that within the individual, an inward struggle. He saw each tragic hero struggling with circumstances and fate, and afflicted with a fatal flaw which causes the tragedy:

> In almost all we observe a marked one-sidedness, a predisposition in some particular direction; a total incapacity, in certain circumstances, of resisting the force which draws in this direction; a fatal tendency to identify the whole being with one interest, object, passion or habit of mind. This, it would seem, is, for Shakespeare, the fundamental tragic trait ... some marked imperfection or defect: irresolution, precipitancy, pride, credulousness, excessive simplicity, excessive susceptibility to sexual emotions and the like ... these contribute decisively to the conflict and catastrophe.

The defect of this aspect of Bradley's approach is evident. Othello does suffer from jealousy, Macbeth from ambition. But those are not their only traits. A consideration of Hamlet quickly shows the range of possible 'flaws' which contribute towards the tragedy: melancholy, hatred of Claudius, incapacity to act, over-thoughtfulness. Hamlet certainly has more than 'one interest, object, passion or habit of mind'. No single formula can sum up the nature of a major character in Shakespearean or Jacobean tragedy. Each is complex, because Shakespeare and the Jacobeans were inventive in their use of a wide variety of language and dramatic devices in creating Hamlet, Lady Macbeth, the Duchess of Malfi or any other tragic character. The emphasis on character also overlooks the social context within which the tragedy occurs, and which is the focus for many contemporary critics.

In his stress on the dramatic function of character, Bradley interpreted the tragedies as stories that reassure the audience or reader. Tragedy is a process which paradoxically, after catastrophe, results in order, unity and goodness. Although the tragedies present conflict and waste, evil is eventually overcome; the ending, if not happy, promises something better ahead. For Bradley, virtue and good triumph in spite of suffering, adversity and death. For example, he argues that *King Lear* ends with

> a sense of law and beauty ... a consciousness of greatness in pain, and
> of solemnity in the mystery we cannot fathom.

Modern critics are sceptical of the optimism of this interpretation and also reject Bradley's view of tragedy as mystical and indescribable ('piteous, fearful and mysterious'). For modern criticism the origins of tragedy lie in identifiable social causes and are capable of being resisted.

▶ Should characters in plays be treated as if they were real human beings? Work with a partner. One of you is passionately committed to Bradley's views, the other equally strongly rejects them. Try to persuade your partner that your view is correct by using examples from the tragedies you know best.

Liberal humanism

Following Bradley, and adopting his major assumptions, the dominant approach to tragedy for much of the 20th century can be called liberal humanist. Liberal humanist critics sought to demonstrate how each tragedy was deeply concerned with morality, showing man (women tended to be overlooked in this criticism) seeking good, but failing in that quest, enduring suffering, but achieving some kind of self-knowledge and spiritual enlightenment. Even though many characters in tragedy seemed to think that life was not worth living, or were convinced of the futility of human existence, the human spirit triumphed over suffering and death. In *The Death of Tragedy*, George Steiner expressed the traditional optimistic interpretation of tragedy:

> There is in the final moments of great tragedy ... a fusion of grief and
> joy, of lament over the fall of man and of rejoicing in the resurrection
> of his spirit.

In such criticism, more significance was given to such speeches as Hamlet's 'What a piece of work is a man! How noble in reason ...', than to the despairing pessimism in his view of the world as 'an unweeded garden', in which only 'rank and gross' things flourish. Liberal humanism emphasised the potential nobility of man over bleaker views of man's nature. It sought to reconcile the reader or spectator to injustice, to flawed human nature, and to pain and suffering as inevitable and beyond human understanding.

This notion that tragedy is somehow mysterious meant that traditional criticism did not challenge, but confirmed the existing social order and conventional beliefs and values. For example, Wilson Knight (1949) saw the death of the tragic hero as the inevitable outcome of some universal but mysterious law. It is a 'riddle of the universe' that defies human comprehension. For Knight, tragedies were like timeless religious or moral tales about the fall of a hero as sacrifice which redeems humanity. The parallels of Knight's interpretation with the story of Jesus are evident.

Even those critics who tried to put the tragedies in the context of Elizabethan and Jacobean England offered views of the times which are now heavily criticised for their simplicity, and neglect of conflict and dissent. Here, the best known critic is E M W Tillyard. His influential book *The Elizabethan World Picture* (1943) portrayed England as unified and harmonious. Tillyard argued that social order was maintained because almost everyone believed in 'the great chain of being'. This was a kind of mental picture which saw everything in its proper place. It applied to nature and to the social world. The sun was at the centre of the universe, the lion dominated over all other beasts, and the monarch was at the top of society. Society worked best when everyone accepted their 'proper' position in the hierarchy. In this view, tragedy arises from the chaos that occurs when the 'natural' order is challenged or overthrown.

In the same way that liberal humanist critics saw unity in society, so too they saw artistic unity in the tragedies. They argued that although the great tragedies of Shakespeare and the Jacobeans portrayed conflict and disruption, they were aesthetically coherent. In their quest for artistic unity, critics searched the tragedies for coherence in themes and imagery. Wilson Knight saw the plays not as realistic dramas, but as explorations of dominant themes, for example the conflict of life and death in *Macbeth*. Caroline Spurgeon in *Shakespeare's Imagery and What it Tells Us* (first published in 1935 and still in print), identified 'image-clusters' as a dominant feature of the plays. She counted the number of times such image-clusters occurred, and argued that they determined the distinctive atmosphere of a play. For example, in *Hamlet* the recurring images of disease and corruption help establish the atmosphere that 'something is rotten in the state of Denmark'.

Within the liberal humanist tradition, other approaches to the tragedies developed. L C Knights' famous essay, 'How many children had Lady Macbeth?' (1933) mocked Bradley's emphasis on character and argued that the plays should be studied for their poetry and language. Another approach urged that attention should focus on Shakespeare's stagecraft: how he responded to the stage techniques and popular tastes of the times. Here, the most notable example is Muriel Bradbrook's *Themes and Conventions of Elizabethan Tragedy* (1935) which shows how characters were created using the conventions of the time, for example, that disguise is impenetrable, motives are unknown, and characters represent particular 'humours' (see the second task below).

▶ Choose any extract from pages 72–97. Suggest briefly how the extract might be interpreted when guided by the approach of each of the following: Bradley (character criticism), Wilson Knight (themes), Spurgeon (imagery), Knights (poetic drama) and Bradbrook (dramatic conventions).

▶ 'Character criticism' sometimes analyses characters using the doctrine of the four humours. This was a popular belief in Jacobean England which claimed there were four fluids (humours) in the body, and that these determined personality. The four humours were blood, phlegm, black bile and 'yellowe', which resulted respectively in characters who are brave ('sanguine'), calm ('phlegmatic'), melancholy ('critical', cynical and dejected) and angry ('choleric'). Some critics argue that playwrights sometimes used the belief to help create characters (for example, the always angry Tybalt in *Romeo and Juliet* is choleric; Hamlet is sanguine but suffers from melancholy, and so on). Consider each character in the tragedy you know best. How far does the belief in humours help explain their personality?

Modern critical approaches

In the second half of the 20th century, more radical approaches increasingly challenged character criticism and liberal humanism. These traditional approaches were seen as concentrating on personal feelings and ignoring history and society. They were criticised for taking a fatalistic view of human existence, implying that men and women are powerless to resist injustice, and that despair and violence are inevitable. Liberal humanism was accused of interpreting tragedy as offering only spiritual comfort. People could at best hope only for becoming reconciled to tragic events; there was no hope of bettering their conditions of life. These assumptions were rejected by the new approaches.

There are a number of different modern approaches to Shakespearean and Jacobean tragedy. Before reading the major contemporary critical perspectives which follow, it is valuable to remind yourself of the table on page 99 which identifies the features that most of them have in common. These may be briefly and differently summarised as: a focus on the social systems which trap individuals in a tragic predicament; a rejection of the inevitability or 'naturalness' of such unjust societies; an invitation to imagine a world where human beings might find justice and equality of rights. The major modern approaches are: political criticism, **feminist criticism, psychoanalytic criticism, deconstruction.**

Political criticism

The most notable early challenge to liberal humanism was made by the Polish critic

Jan Kott. He fought with the Polish army and underground movement against the Nazis in the Second World War (1939–1945), and had direct experience of the suffering and terror caused by Stalinist repression in Poland in the years after the war. Kott's book *Shakespeare our Contemporary* (1965) saw parallels between the violence and cruelty of the modern world and the worlds of tyranny and despair that Shakespeare depicted in his tragedies. The importance of the title of Kott's book cannot be overstressed. It emphasises that Shakespeare is modern in his bleak view of human history and humanity itself.

Kott argues that history, rather than fate or the gods, is the cause of tragedy. He uses the image of 'the Grand Mechanism' of history: a great staircase up which characters tread to their doom, each step 'marked by murder, perfidy, treachery'. It does not matter if a character is good or bad, history will overwhelm them. Characters have little or no power over their lives, but are swept aside by inevitable social and historical forces beyond their control.

In this grim scenario of history, Kott equates *King Lear* with Beckett's *Endgame*: a play whose grotesque ending produces no catharsis. For him the Murderers in *Richard III* 'are just cog-wheels of the Grand Mechanism'. Hamlet is not a romantic character, but a despairing modern man; Fortinbras is 'the man of the strong arm' who takes over at the end, with historic inevitability. Kott sees Macbeth's ordering the murder of Banquo as 'the Auschwitz experience', a reminder of the Nazi death camps. The play itself is nihilistic:

> The very concept of man has crumbled to pieces, and there is nothing left … Macbeth does not feel guilty … All he can do before he dies is to drag with him into nothingness as many living beings as possible. This is the last consequence of the world's absurdity.

Kott's book, although today much criticised by later critics, can be seen as the forerunner of new approaches which focus on the social and political contexts and causes of tragedy. For example, J W Lever in *The Tragedy of State* (1971) firmly rejects the focus on the tragic hero in favour of concentration on the society in which he exists. For Lever, tragedy

> is not primarily treatments of characters with a so-called 'fatal flaw', whose downfall is brought about by the decree of just if inscrutable powers … the fundamental flaw is in the world they inhabit: in the political state, the social order it upholds … In Jacobean tragedy it is not primarily the conduct of the individual, but of the society which assails him, that stands condemned.

Jonathan Dollimore in a key book, *Radical Tragedy* (1989), similarly rejects the traditional focus on the tragic hero. He also argues that criticism should centre instead upon society, and the subjects of his own analysis are utterly clear:

> ... issues of class, sexuality, imperialist and colonial exploitation have everything to do with Jacobean tragedy.

Dollimore has no doubt about the relationships between the tragedies and the state. He claims that in those plays, Shakespeare and the Jacobean playwrights actively question and subvert contemporary political power and ideology. For Dollimore, the tragedies display 'a kind of intellectual vandalism' because they expose the injustices and inequalities of Elizabethan and Jacobean society, and they question the beliefs and structures which maintain those unfair practices.

Dollimore argues that traditional criticism is misleading because it claims that the tragedies reflect Elizabethan and Jacobean England as a contented, integrated world. He rejects as false the Elizabethan world picture which presented the universe and society as naturally ordered and hierarchical. Dollimore sees this belief used by those in power to justify and maintain monarchical rule in which Elizabeth or James and a small number of aristocrats enjoyed huge power and privilege.

Dollimore is similarly critical of traditional criticism which saw tragedy being about aesthetics (the study of the beautiful in art), rather than about social reality. The aesthetic approach sees tragedy as ultimately about finding order and universal truths in the conflict and suffering of tragedy. For Dollimore, all these artistic aims remove literature from its social and political context. In contrast, he claims that Jacobean tragedy is not about order, but disorder, and the plays make visible the power struggles within Jacobean society.

Dollimore agrees with Karl Marx that religion is 'the opium of people', a control drug that removes any desire to protest or act against injustice and inequality. He endorses Richard III's view that conscience 'is but a word that cowards use,/ Devised at first to keep the strong in awe', and claims that in Shakespeare's England religious considerations were giving way to political and economic pressures. The tragedies reveal that change by showing the real nature of power behind the religious justifications that were given (see 'divine right of kings', page 31):

> ... in the Renaissance God was in trouble ... Jacobean plays provoke by revealing as social, political and historical what prevailing authorities would legitimate metaphysically.

Dollimore's attack on character criticism is equally fundamental. He challenges the 'central assumptions of the traditional reading of character, human nature and individual identity' of traditional criticism. For Dollimore, human personality is determined by, and reflects the historical conditions of the time. It is not stable or unified, but fractured and full of contradictions. He argues that unstable concept of man is expressed in the malcontents of tragedy: Iago, Edmund, and the vengeful, satirical, dispossessed anti-heroes of Jacobean tragedy. Such men are both the victims and the agents of social corruption, and reveal the true nature of society:

> ... the Jacobean malcontent ... is not the antithesis of social process but its focus ... the focus of political, social, and ideological contradiction.

The two major schools of political criticism are **new historicism** (largely American), and **cultural materialism** (largely British). Their assumptions are virtually the same, but new historicism focuses on the Elizabethan and Jacobean period. Its best-known practitioner, Stephen Greenblatt, argues that the authorities of the time permitted tragedies to be performed, even if they criticised the state, because the effect was to contain and reduce such criticism. After all, the tragedies end with the challenges to authority contained and with the same hierarchical system firmly in place. Only the persons have changed. At the end of *Hamlet*, Fortinbras becomes the new, even more powerful ruler of Denmark.

Cultural materialism is more concerned with today's world. It is a way of reading tragedy that argues that culture (in all its forms, including tragedy) and materialism (economic factors) are always related. Interpretations of the tragedies are shaped by the economic, political and ideological (belief) systems of the times. Cultural materialism is also openly political in its purpose. Two of its leading advocates, Jonathan Dollimore and Alan Sinfield, in their book *Political Shakespeare* (1994), declare that their style of criticism is not politically neutral, but is committed to 'the transformation of a social order which exploits people on grounds of race, gender and class'.

Modern political criticism argues that traditional approaches have always interpreted tragedies conservatively, in ways that confirm and maintain the interests of the elite, dominant class. For example, traditional criticism asserts that *Macbeth* is 'a study in evil'. But political criticism claims that 'evil' is a mystification, a concept which deflects attention away from social factors: the oppressive, feudal militaristic structure of Scotland. That, rather than the supernatural or witchcraft is a more powerful and truthful approach to understanding the tragedy.

In the same way, political approaches argue that *Hamlet* is best studied as a society in the process of change. Denmark has moved from the stability of feudal chivalry to a troubled and unsettled world. In these changed times Hamlet finds himself adrift and powerless, unable to rely on older certainties. There are no longer clear answers to the questions that afflict him: revenge, suicide, the nature of ghosts, salvation. Similarly *The Duchess of Malfi* shows how a woman whose values and behaviour are ahead of her time is trapped and destroyed by the male dominated values and power of a feudal world.

▶ Consider the two tragedies you know best. Describe the society in which each is set. In what ways are they similar? How far do you consider each society to be responsible for the deaths that occur?

▶ Read the extract from *Richard II* on pages 77–78. Step into role as a modern political critic and give your response to Richard's description of England.

Most radical critics avoid speculating about Shakespeare's own politics or his intentions in writing his tragedies. But one Marxist critic, Victor Kiernan, attempts to root the tragedies squarely in Shakespeare's own experience of life in Elizabethan and Jacobean England. In *Eight Tragedies of Shakespeare: A Marxist Study* (1996), Kiernan argues that Shakespeare's concern was for the poor whose toil and suffering pays for the pleasures and follies of the rich, and that he was haunted by the image of the poor man in the stocks. Kiernan thinks that Shakespeare's tragic vision

> must have started from something personal, some dislocation of his own life ... which opened his eyes wider to the world round him and to its martyrdom.

Kiernan's assumption results in social interpretations. He claims that Hamlet is 'Shakespeare's spokesman for common humanity ... and ... is in the process of growing aware of hardship and exploitation in the life around him'. He sees in Hamlet's 'O what a rogue and peasant slave am I' soliloquy 'a reminder of how English ploughmen were being degraded into a dispirited race of hired labourers'.

In the harsh world of *King Lear*, Kiernan sees a reflection of the ruthlessness of the Jacobean age. An older, more stable age has passed, and now 'men are as the time is', pitiless and self-seeking. He argues that although the play shows very little of the hungry poor, and nothing of riotous crowds:

> Shakespeare works on our imagination instead, keeping the poor an invisible but compelling presence ... Shakespeare leaves us to hope that some day the masses will stand up for themselves.

▶ Do you believe, like Kiernan, that Shakespeare's (or Webster's or Middleton's) own political beliefs are expressed in the tragedies? Select four or five quotations from one play and argue for and against the view that they are the playwright's own beliefs.

Feminist criticism

This is the fastest growing and most widespread of all modern approaches to tragedy. Feminist criticism opposes the maleness of traditional criticism written by men and which often stereotypes or distorts the woman's point of view. This 'male ownership' of criticism meant that it was men who determined what questions were to be asked of a play, and which answers were acceptable. In contrast, feminists examine how female experience is portrayed in criticism of tragedy, and expose how women's feelings and actions are neglected, repressed or misrepresented.

Feminist criticism is part of the wider project of feminism, which aims to achieve rights and equality for women in social, political and economic life. It challenges sexism: those beliefs and practices which result in the oppression and subordination of women. Feminism reveals how gender roles are shaped to the disadvantage of women in family, work, politics and religion. It exposes the male prejudice which for millennia has portrayed women as different from and inferior to men (remind yourself of John Knox' 1558 description of women on page 28).

The feminist approach shows how such negative perception of women is evident in tragedy. Male language in the tragedies frequently demeans women. Hamlet's 'Frailty, thy name is woman' summarises John Knox' misogynistic male view. Cleopatra is described as a 'dish', 'morsel', 'fragment', 'boggler', and 'like a cow in June'. Witches are demonised, and Lady Macbeth is portrayed as the embodiment of evil.

The portrayal of women in the tragedies reflects the realities of the limited power and status of women in Elizabethan and Jacobean England. Feminist criticism reveals how social anxieties are displaced on to sexuality, giving rise to the concern about 'troublesome women': scolds, witches, or any female who posed a threat to male authority. It points out for example that in Jacobean tragedy women are typically victims, but in traditional criticism strong women are demonised or disvalued.

In Jacobean tragedies women are often seen as the focus of all ills. In the view of dominant males in the plays, women are the source of lust, they subvert male power, and their influence results in chaos. But they are destroyed by the end of the tragedy, and have no part in the new order. Feminist criticism highlights the hypocrisy of two brothers of the Duchess of Malfi who condemn her sexuality. It identifies how, in *Women Beware Women*, Bianca is at the mercy of whims of her husband and her lover; and in *The White Devil*, how male prejudice ensures Vittoria does not get a fair trial.

Hamlet's mother, Gertrude, is the focus for much feminist criticism. Compared with the men, she has comparatively few lines. But Claudius, the Ghost and Hamlet all seem obsessed with her as sex object, and Hamlet's feelings for her are expressed in a combination of violence and disgust. Feminist critics point out that much traditional criticism has adopted this male viewpoint, and that it is also reflected in film portrayals of Gertrude. They argue that both Olivier's 1948 and the Russian Kozintsev's 1964 films portray Hamlet's view of his mother, showing Gertrude as lascivious, vain, and self-satisfied. Such interpretations neglect what Gertrude is as created by her own words: a loving, caring mother and wife.

▶ Read the extracts from *Hamlet* and *The White Devil* on pages 80, 90. How do the men regard the women in those extracts? If you were directing the plays and wished to present each scene from a female viewpoint, how would you stage them?

Feminist approaches to tragedy vary widely because there is of course more than one 'woman's point of view'. But a key feminist critic, Jacqueline Dusinberre, in *Shakespeare and the Nature of Women* (1996) claims that 'drama from 1590 to 1625 is feminist in sympathy'. She points out that plays could express ideas not tolerated elsewhere, and argues strongly that Shakespeare challenges traditional ideas of women as a different and inferior species:

> Shakespeare saw men and women as equal in a world which declared them as unequal. He did not divide human nature into the masculine and the feminine, but observed in the individual woman or man an infinite variety of union between opposing impulses ... he refused to separate their worlds physically, intellectually or spiritually.

Other feminist critics do not share Dusinberre's view that Jacobean tragedy is 'feminist in sympathy', and seek to expose the misogyny (hatred of women) and patriarchy (male domination) that degrades women in the tragedies. But all share the common aim of demonstrating the vital contribution that the female characters contribute to the plays (for example, how Desdemona, Emilia and Bianca shape the conflicts, themes and plot of *Othello*). Given that common purpose, different feminist critics focus on different aspects of tragedy:

- family relationships: for example, Lear, like many other Shakespearean fathers, is enraged when his daughters disobey him

- positive views of women: how some women resist, trying to establish an equal place in the male world of the tragedies, for example Vittoria in *The White Devil*, the Duchess of Malfi, Cleopatra, Lady Macbeth, Gonerill and Regan

- the bravery of women: for example, how the heroines of Jacobean tragedy boldly face death, and how Shakespeare's youngest heroine, Juliet, fearlessly kills herself for love

- how the tragedies invite dissent from misogyny and patriarchy: for example, how the plays can be interpreted and performed in ways that expose patriarchy as vicious and unjust
- men's inability to reconcile tender affection with sexual desire
- how particular kinds of masculinity cause the tragedy: for example, the military macho world of *Othello*, obsessed with spurious notions of male honour
- women as property: the major female characters in Jacobean tragedy are regarded as male possessions, subject to disposal as men think fit
- women's relations to each other: for example, sisterhoods of resistance or female friendship (Desdemona and Emilia; Gonerill and Regan; Cleopatra, Charmian and Iras; the three queens in *Richard III*; the compassionate female attendants in Jacobean tragedies); the absence of a female sub-culture in *Macbeth*, *Hamlet* and *Romeo and Juliet* (Lady Macbeth, Gertrude and Ophelia appear always with men, and Juliet must face her greatest test alone).

Feminist critics challenge the traditional portrayal of women as examples of 'virtue' or 'vice'. In arguing for equality, feminists demonstrate that Desdemona is not a saint, nor Lady Macbeth a monster. They are, like the male characters, complex and flawed, experiencing similar emotions to men and suffering like them. In *Othello*, Emilia's tolerant, practical words have been taken as a feminist manifesto for equality with men:

> Let husbands know
> Their wives have sense like them: they see and smell,
> And have their palates both for sweet and sour
> As husbands have. What is it that they do
> When they change us for others? Is it sport?
> I think it is. And doth affection breed it?
> I think it doth. Is't frailty that thus errs?
> It is so too. And have we not affections,
> Desires for sport, and frailty, as men have?
> Then let them use us well; else let them know
> The ills we do, their ills instruct us so.

▶ Choose the tragedy you know best. How would you describe its presentation of the women? For example, is it sympathetic, or critical, or ...? Use evidence from the play to support your views.

Psychoanalytic criticism

In the 20th century, psychoanalysis became a major influence on the understanding and interpretation of human behaviour. The founder of psychoanalysis, Sigmund Freud, explained personality as the result of unconscious and irrational desires, repressed memories or wishes, sexuality, fantasy, anxiety and conflict. Freud's theories, together with his stress on early childhood experiences, have strongly influenced criticism and stagings of tragedy. In schools, a popular classroom activity is 'put a character on the psychiatrist's couch'.

Freud's interpretation of dreams provides a key to the psychoanalytic approach. Freud distinguished between what he called 'manifest content' and 'latent content' of dreams: the obvious story versus the hidden story, the explicit versus the implicit meaning of a tragic story. This seems very like the conventional distinction between text and sub-text (behind the surface meaning of language and action lies a deeper meaning). But psychoanalysis is distinctive in that it interprets the deeper meaning as some personal trauma or anxiety, often sexual, in experience and relationships.

Psychoanalytic criticism has particular relevance to the macabre worlds of Jacobean tragedy with their sexually obsessed, violent and irrational characters. In *The Duchess of Malfi*, Duke Ferdinand imagines himself to be a wolf, and is often interpreted as having incestuous desire for his sister the Duchess. For Shakespeare, psychoanalysis has yielded some readings which have become familiar and much-discussed interpretations. Coriolanus' bond with his mother undoubtedly leads to his destruction. Most famously, Laurence Olivier's 1948 film of *Hamlet*, heavily influenced by psychoanalytic theory, suggests that Hamlet suffers from the Oedipus complex (the desire to kill his father and sleep with his mother). Since then it has become conventional to argue that Hamlet possesses strong sexual feelings towards Gertrude.

Other critics have speculated about the family history of the Macbeths (did they or did they not have children?), and the childhood experiences of Lear's three daughters (Jane Smiley's novel *A Thousand Acres* is a modern imaginative exploration of that experience). A glimpse of Hamlet's childhood is shown in Kenneth Branagh's 1997 film of *Hamlet*. But some psychoanalytic claims have provoked startled or hostile reaction, for example the claim that Othello secretly desires Cassio, or that Iago has repressed homosexual feelings for Othello, or that the Ghost in *Hamlet* represents the phallus.

Psychoanalytic approaches have obvious weaknesses. They cannot be proved or disproved, they neglect historical and social factors, and they often impose meaning from psychoanalytic theory rather than from the text. Nonetheless, psychoanalysis seems well suited to tragedy, because it shares a similar subject matter: love and hate, dreams, fantasy and confusion. Tragedy and psychoanalysis are deeply concerned with personal and family relationships as the root of disruption. In

Shakespeare's tragedies many conflicts spring from fathers' desire to control their daughters' lives: Lear, Capulet, Desdemona, Ophelia. Similarly, Jacobean tragedy portrays deeply dysfunctional families: the Duchess of Malfi's cruel brothers; the incestuous sister-brother love of *'Tis Pity She's a Whore*; the mother willing to consent to the seduction of her daughter in *The White Devil*, and the brother who would similarly sell his sister in *The Revenger's Tragedy*.

▶ Choose a character. Step into role as a psychoanalyst and write a report on your character, using only evidence you can find in the text.

Deconstruction

Deconstruction has two applications to tragedy. The first is straightforward and familiar. It involves 'taking the play apart' to see how it works, how it 'fits together'. This is little more than traditional studies of language, character and story. It involves, for example, showing how puns and ambiguity add to the richness of possible meanings; or telling how characters relate to each other; or analysing how one section of the story is connected to what follows. These are familiar and common-sense practices.

The second application of deconstruction is much more challenging. It takes several forms:

- In its most extreme form, deconstruction claims that it is impossible to find any meaning in language, because words simply refer to other words, and so any interpretation is endlessly delayed (or 'deferred' as the deconstructionists say). But this type of deconstruction is self-contradictory, because there would be no point in writing books on deconstruction if communication was impossible. It therefore has little or no value for students beginning a study of tragedy.

- Another radical type of deconstruction asserts that human beings have no essential identity. This is similar to the view held by Jonathan Dollimore (see pages 104–106) who argues that characters in the tragedies (and people in real life) are shaped by historical and social forces. The problem with such an approach is that it reduces characters to puppets dancing on the strings of history, and it denies the value of speaking of someone (in tragedies or in life) as 'consumed with jealousy', or 'full of hatred', or 'driven by ambition', etc. In practice, deconstructive readings of this type demonstrate little more than that the major characters in tragedy are complex, full of conflicting impulses, feelings and thoughts (rather like most human beings).

- The most common type of deconstructive approach is that which produces readings 'to show what is really going on'. In practice, this is often little more than revealing the sub-text, the deeper meanings that lie behind surface meanings or appearances. Where it becomes controversial is when the deconstruction interpretation claims to reveal meanings that challenge traditional readings, as for example in Terry Eagleton's claim that the witches are the heroines of *Macbeth*. In practice, many political, feminist and psychoanalytic interpretations can be claimed as examples of deconstruction because of the strong disagreement they provoke. For this reason deconstruction is often called 'reading against the grain' or less politely 'textual harassment'.

- Another form of deconstruction focuses on the contradictions and absurdities in tragedy, or on minor or marginal characters, or on gaps or silences in the play. Here the claim of deconstruction is that these features, previously overlooked as unimportant, reveal significant truths about the play. Examples of this approach are common in school classrooms when students tell the story of the tragedy from the point of view of a minor character (for example, a servant in Macbeth's castle), or parody a speech, or brings to life an 'absent' character (who is mentioned, but never appears).

- Yet another form of deconstruction can be called 'postmodernism' (which means little more than 'a mixture of styles'). This approach does not attempt to tell a coherent story, or to create consistent characters, but accepts all kinds of anomalies and contradictions in a spirit of playfulness or 'carnival'. In criticism it means not being concerned to develop a reasoned argument (and therefore has drawbacks for examination students!). It is most clearly seen in practice in stage productions which dress characters in costumes from very different historical periods, or use modern and ancient weapons simultaneously, or which end very ambiguously.

▶ Read Richard III's speech as he wakes from his dream before the Battle of Bosworth (see the extract on pages 75–77). Deconstruction interprets this as a demonstration of his 'disintegrated identity' ('My conscience hath a thousand several tongues'). Write your own interpretation of what the speech reveals about Richard.

Assignments

1 Work in a group of five. You are about to stage the extract from *Hamlet* (page 80). But each of you wishes to stage it guided by different critical approaches (Bradley, political, feminist, psychoanalytic, deconstructive). Each person presents their proposal to the group, and invites discussion.

2 Turn to pages 109–110 and remind yourself of the list of topics that feminist critics have investigated. Choose one topic (or a topic of your choice) and research it in a number of Shakespearean and Jacobean tragedies.

3   Is a character in tragedy like a real person? Choose a male and a female character and write about the advantages and disadvantages of seeing them as living persons.

4   Hamlet claimed that the purpose of theatre is, and always has been, to portray and comment critically upon the times

    ... the purpose of playing, whose end both at the first and now, was and is, to hold as 'twere the mirror up to nature; to show virtue her own feature, scorn her own image, and the very age and body of the time his form and pressure ...

    Choose one tragedy and describe how you would stage it to fulfil Hamlet's purposes.

5   Imagine you are a film director. You are about to begin work on filming a Shakespearean or Jacobean tragedy. Choose your play and write an account of how you propose to film it, influenced by your knowledge of critical writing about tragedy.

6   Identify and compare the imagery used in one Shakespearean and one Jacobean tragedy. How does the imagery help establish the tragic atmosphere of each play?

7   Some critics argue that staging a tragedy in the theatre or on film is a political activity, because all artistic activity is heavily influenced by social factors. Give your own response to that view by considering productions you have seen on stage or film.

8   'A tragedy is like a mirror. It reflects back the preoccupations of the reader or spectator. Whatever you are interested in - politics, psychology, sexuality, class, culture - you will find it in the tragedy you are watching or studying.' How far do you agree with this claim? Use your own responses to one or more tragedies to illustrate your reply.

6 | How to write about Shakespearean and Jacobean tragedy

- How can the concept of 'tragedy' help your writing?

- How can the notion of 'public and personal' help your writing?

- What other approaches can help your writing about tragedy?

- How far will your own views be influenced by the interpretations of others?

The concept of 'tragedy'

How do you respond to a tragedy by Shakespeare or a Jacobean playwright? For example, do you believe that the deaths of Romeo and Juliet end the feud of the Montagues and Capulets and reconcile the two families? Or do you think that the feud will continue, and the deaths of the two young lovers resolve nothing? Is the ending of *King Lear* utterly negative and bleak, or does it hold out some promise of hope? Why is the innocent Duchess of Malfi so cruelly oppressed by her brothers? Just what is rotten in the state of Denmark?

The first thing to be said is that there is no single or 'right' way to respond to, or write about tragedy. Part 5 has shown some of the very different ways in which Shakespearean and Jacobean tragedy has been discussed and written about by critics. What is important is that you give your personal response to what you read or what you see on stage or film, and that you show as clearly as possible why you think and feel as you do. You should, of course, support your interpretation with evidence from the text, but the fact that you are studying a tragedy can be a great help to your writing.

As has been shown in earlier sections, 'tragedy' is a genre, a particular kind of writing. That means that every tragedy shares distinctive characteristics: the drama will concern suffering and death, and the dominant mood will be serious or sombre. Keeping these characteristics in mind will enable you to organise your responses. For example, for each play you need to ask yourself two basic questions:

- Who is (or are) the major tragic character (or characters)?

- What makes them tragic?

The first question is usually easy to answer. There is always one or more 'tragic heroes', and they may be male or female. The second question gives you a way of organising your written response as you analyse the nature of the characters' suffering: what happens to them in the course of the play. Your analysis is more than simply a retelling of events, because it recognises that tragedy is about waste and loss. In every tragedy something precious is lost, most obviously life itself, but other desirable valued aspects of human life too.

Consider some examples. Juliet, Richard II and the Duchess of Malfi lose their lives, but in each case the tragedy is intensified by their loss of other precious things. Juliet loses Romeo, love, youth, family, her trust in the Nurse. Richard II loses his crown, wealth and status, and his poetic lyricism. The Duchess loses husband, children, status, and her essential innocence and goodness die with her.

Your writing identifies what a character once possessed, and how the tragedy of the play deprives them of all those precious things. Each item of 'loss' can be discussed with reference to the text, to show how the playwright makes the audience aware of what is wasted by the tragedy. The sense of loss is evident in particular speeches:

> Oh what a noble mind is here o'erthrown!
> The courtier's, soldier's, scholar's, eye, tongue, sword,
> Th'expectancy and rose of the fair state,
> The glass of fashion and the mould of form,
> Th'observed of all observers, quite, quite down,
> And I of ladies most deject and wretched,
> That sucked the honey of his music vows,
> Now see that noble and most sovereign reason,
> Like sweet bells jangled, out of tune and harsh;
> That unmatched form and feature of blown youth
> Blasted with ecstasy. O woe is me
> T'have seen what I have seen, see what I see.

Ophelia has just been the victim of Hamlet's verbal abuse. Her speech displays tragedy's sense of waste as she lists what has been lost in Hamlet's transformation. Each of her first five lines includes one or more of the qualities of a great person ('noble mind', 'expectancy and rose of the fair state', etc.). But all those desirable features are gone: 'quite, quite down', 'Blasted with ecstasy'. There is an overwhelming impression of the wasting of excellence and promise.

▶ Choose one tragic character. What does he or she lose in the tragedy? How does the playwright help the audience experience a sense of loss?

Public and personal: focus on society and individual

Another characteristic of tragedy that can help your writing is that every tragic hero is caught up in a particular social or political setting. Public matters shape the actions and responses of individuals, and individual actions have consequences for the state. That relationship of private and public matters is sometimes embodied in the title of the play: *King Richard III*; *Othello, the Moor of Venice*; *Hamlet, Prince of Denmark*. Hamlet's challenge to Claudius is both personal and political. Through Claudius' actions, Hamlet has lost not only his father and mother, but also crown and country. His vow of revenge will directly affect the state of Denmark.

Like all other tragic heroes, Hamlet's personal feelings and moral choices have social implications. Even Juliet, a 13-year-old girl with no political or social power, finds herself constrained by social expectations and values. She is expected to be a dutiful daughter and a Capulet, but those social obligations clash with her personal feelings for Romeo, a Montague.

Ophelia is another young powerless female, but her speech shows how the public and the private are indissolubly bound up together. The tragic reading on page 116 can be discussed from different standpoints, and in your writing it is helpful to show awareness that both 'public' (social and political) and 'personal' (character) interpretations are possible. The first is concerned with a social reading of Ophelia's speech, the second with character.

- Public interpretation
  A social or political reading would discuss the many references to the qualities embodied in a ruler of an ordered, chivalrous society. The hopes and values of that state are represented in the monarch. Their overthrow results in chaos. Feminist readings are also social readings. Here, such an interpretation puts the speech in the context of Ophelia's encounter with Hamlet in the 'nunnery' scene. He insults and demeans her and all women, repudiating their past relationship, leaving her 'deject and wretched'. But even in this betrayal, Ophelia still expresses male qualities as the supreme virtues for leadership of the state.

- Personal interpretation
  Here you would discuss character, the distressed state of Ophelia's mind, her description of herself as 'most deject and wretched', and the hint that Hamlet's derangement ('Blasted with ecstasy') may be a hint of her future descent into madness. But your writing should identify how both levels, public and private, are related. The two characters, Hamlet and Ophelia, are caught up in a hierarchical society that values order and kingship, but in which power is based on murder, force and spying. Those social conditions affect individual actions and perceptions. Each tragedy is a tale of destructive relationships within unjust societies where tragic characters lose love, integrity, honour, even identity itself.

Writing at these two levels, personal and public, can help you with a key question for all tragedies: 'What causes the tragedy?' For example, with *Macbeth*, at the level of the individual, you can write about Macbeth's character, that he is consumed with ambition to become king. Or, at the public level, you can discuss the rigid social setting of the play, feudal Scotland, male and military, where fighting is a way of life, and competing warlords struggle ruthlessly for power.

For many tragedies there is a third focus for your writing. It discusses the supernatural or metaphysical aspects of the play, for example seeing the witches as superhuman beings (supernatural), or using such expressions as '*Macbeth* is a study in evil' (metaphysical) which claims that the most significant aspect of *Macbeth* is the metaphysical concept of evil, which causes and pervades the whole tragedy. These kinds of explanation have fallen out of favour in recent years, and many critics regard them as mystifications because they obscure the social and political shaping of tragic events. Nonetheless, you can see how different levels of explanation operate by considering the answer to the question 'Why did Romeo and Juliet die?'

- Personal interpretation (about the psychology of character)
  They die because of their rashness, or the anger of Capulet, or the scheming of Friar Lawrence, etc.

- Public interpretation (about the type of society in which the tragedy is set)
  They die because they are caught between two factions (the Montagues and Capulets, each with their own notions of honour and revenge) struggling for power in the divided city of Verona. A different kind of social explanation is given by feminism: they die because of patriarchy - the male desire for dominance.

- Metaphysical interpretation
  Such explanations argue that the tragedy is explained by causes that lie outside human control. Here for example Romeo and Juliet's tragedy is caused by 'fate' or 'Fortune': the malign influence of the stars; bad luck; chance or accident.

Obviously, the most effective writing discusses the links between all three levels, showing that they all influence each other and are in necessarily complex relationship. You may believe that one level of interpretation is more important than the others, but you need to show your awareness of other kinds of explanation, and present evidence that both supports and challenges your own preferences.

▶ Choose any extract from pages 72–97. Write two interpretations, one focusing on character, the other at the social and political level. Add a third interpretation (metaphysical or supernatural) if you think it appropriate.

Other focuses for your writing: language, themes, contexts, stagecraft

You can of course concentrate on other aspects of tragedy in your writing. For example, the critic Frank Kermode in *Shakespeare's Language* (2000) urges close attention to how playwrights use language to poetic and dramatic effect and to establish character and atmosphere. Here, your discussion would include examples of imagery, techniques of repetition and key words (for example 'blood' in *Macbeth*, 'natural' in *King Lear*, 'honest' in *Othello*).

Such a reading of Ophelia's speech would discuss the rich imagery, the frequent use of doubling ('expectancy and rose', 'the glass of fashion and the mould of form', 'deject and wretched', 'noble and most sovereign reason', 'out of time and harsh', 'unmatched form and feature') and the repetitions and lists ('courtier's, soldier's, scholar's', 'observed/observers' 'seen/seen', 'see/see').

► Select one extract from pages 72–97. Write an account of its language to show how the playwright creates character, atmosphere and dramatic effect.

Or you might choose an approach that concentrates on the themes of the tragedy you are studying. All Shakespearean and Jacobean tragedies share certain common themes, notably appearance and reality, order and disorder, conflict and change (or 'corruption' for Jacobean tragedies, see pages 11, 29–30 and 60). Many plays have 'revenge' as a central theme, but every play has its own distinctive interests or preoccupations which become a mainspring for the tragedy: 'ambition' (*Macbeth*), 'jealousy' (*Othello*), 'pride' (*Coriolanus*) and so on.

As you can see, themes are usually expressed as abstract nouns (like the ones in the preceding paragraphs, and others such as 'honour', 'patriarchy', 'justice', 'madness' and so on). Such abstractions are a major way of explaining what a play is about, but in every case your writing needs to include evidence of the particularity of the play: its unique language, characters and story.

For example, when Capulet rages at his daughter 'I'll give you to my friend', his words are a vivid illustration of patriarchy: as a father he treats Juliet like an object, something he can give away to whoever he likes. When Iago says 'I am not what I am', or Lady Macbeth advises 'Look like th'innocent flower, but be the serpent under't', their words strikingly embody the theme of reality and appearance. And every Jacobean tragedy contains many lines in which characters call for revenge (as when, in *The Revenger's Tragedy*, Vindice's brother congratulates him 'I do applaud thy constant vengeance').

► Choose one tragedy and identify its major themes. Find short quotations to illustrate each theme.

A further focus for your writing can be the central topic of this book: what Shakespearean and Jacobean tragedies reveal about the social and cultural aspects of their times. The various features of Elizabethan and Jacobean England set out in Part 2 (pages 15–39) can all be identified in many of the tragedies. They are both sources for the playwright's imagination, and examples of, or comments on, contemporary events or conditions. You can use the various topics discussed in Part 2 to structure your writing. Some topics are clearly present in every tragedy, most obviously beliefs about women, hierarchy in society and nature, and religion (although, of course, taking different expression in each play). These, and other influences on particular plays discussed in Part 3 can provide the basis for your own research to help your writing.

▶ Choose one extract from pages 72–97. What does it reveal about beliefs, attitudes or practices of the time when it was written?

Whatever the focus of your writing, always keep in mind that Shakespeare and the Jacobean playwrights wrote plays. They intended their tragedies to be performed on stage, in front of an audience. So attention to the writer's stagecraft will improve your own writing. This means considering the theatrical qualities of the tragedies; the dramatic effects produced by means other than language, characters or ideas. Aspects of stagecraft which give the play its impact on stage include opportunities for spectacle, timing, tension, contrast, the presentation of conflict and passion, climax and anticlimax, dramatic irony and discrepant awareness (where one character knows more than another).

For example, if you are writing about an extract from a tragedy, your discussion of the dramatic significance of the passage should attempt to visualise it in performance. This means placing the passage in the context of the whole play, and discussing how speeches are delivered (tone, pauses, emphases). It also includes considering who is on stage, how they interrelate, how they react to what is said, the tensions and moods generated, climactic moments, and the possibilities for conflict in the episode. You would go on to consider the effects such stagecraft might have on the audience, in Shakespeare's time and today.

▶ Choose the tragedy you feel you know best. Turn to the final scene. Use the two paragraphs above to help you identify the elements of stagecraft which ensure that the scene has a significant effect on the audience.

What account should you take of critics?

Very different interpretations have been offered by critics over time, and as Part 5 has shown, critics today discuss the tragedies from competing points of view (feminist, psychoanalytic, etc.). Some knowledge of those different interpretations and approaches can help you shape your own responses. But please don't think that you have to read every critic (that's impossible, there are simply far too many!). And don't think that you have to agree with any particular critical interpretation. Indeed, it is usually best to argue with an interpretation to show how the interpretation has made you think about your own views, confirming them or modifying them in some way. In this way your writing is a dialogue with the tragedy you are studying and a dialogue with other readers of that tragedy whose views may or may not coincide with your own.

Assignments

1 Tragedy conveys a sense of loss or waste. Choose any extract from pages 72–97 and discuss in what ways it transmits a feeling of loss or waste.

2 Find a critical account of the tragedy you know best. Summarise what you think are the critic's major perceptions of the play. Then compare those views with your own interpretations, identifying how far you agree or disagree with the critic.

3 Theatre and acting provided a rich source of imagery for Shakespeare and the Jacobean playwrights. Acting is about pretence and deception, so it lends itself perfectly to the falseness or hypocrisy of the villains of the tragedies. In the play you are studying, find images based on theatre and acting. Suggest how they illustrate the theme of appearance and reality.

4 Select one play and use the model given for *Romeo and Juliet* on page 118 to write an account of the causes of the tragedy.

5 Choose one aspect of Elizabethan and Jacobean society (as listed on pages 23–38). Show how it is reflected in two or more tragedies.

6 Compare the final scene of one Shakespearean and one Jacobean tragedy. What features does each 'ending' have in common?

7 Step into role as a theatre director. You are about to direct a tragedy of your choice. Write the talk you will give to your cast at your first rehearsal meeting. It will give your view of the distinctive features of the language of the play, and how those features will help your actors' performances.

7 | Resources

Chronology

Insufficient evidence means that it is impossible to give precise dates for when the tragedies discussed in this book were written. The following are dates generally agreed by scholars, but they should be treated with caution as only approximate.

1587	Christopher Marlowe *Tamburlaine the Great, Parts 1 and 2*
1589	Thomas Kyd *The Spanish Tragedy* Christopher Marlowe *Doctor Faustus*
1590	Christopher Marlowe *The Jew of Malta*
1592	William Shakespeare *Titus Andronicus*
1592–1593	William Shakespeare *King Richard III*
1594	William Shakespeare *King Richard II*
1595	William Shakespeare *Romeo and Juliet*
1599	William Shakespeare *Julius Caesar*
1601	William Shakespeare *Hamlet*
1603	death of Queen Elizabeth I, accession of King James 1 (start of 'the Jacobean period')
1604	William Shakespeare *Othello*
1605	William Shakespeare *King Lear* Thomas Middleton *The Revenger's Tragedy* (once thought to be written by Cyril Tourneur)
1606	William Shakespeare *Macbeth*; *Antony and Cleopatra*
1607	William Shakespeare *Coriolanus*
1608	William Shakespeare *Timon of Athens*
1612	John Webster *The White Devil*
1614	John Webster *The Duchess of Malfi*
1616	death of William Shakespeare
1622	Thomas Middleton *The Changeling*
1624	Thomas Middleton *Women Beware Women*
1625	death of King James I

Further reading

It is easy to feel overwhelmed by the sheer number of books written about Shakespeare and the Jacobean playwrights. But don't feel daunted. The following publications are particularly relevant to the focus of this book, and all are available either in bookshops or through your school, college or local library.

The tragedies in the context of their times

G Blakemore Evans *Elizabethan-Jacobean Drama* (A & C Black, 1987)
An excellent collection of original documents and pictures which illuminate the social and theatrical contexts of the tragedies.

A R Braunmuller and Michael Hattaway, eds. *The Cambridge Companion to English Renaissance Drama* (Cambridge University Press, 1990)
The chapter by Robert N Watson on 'Tragedy' is very helpful, and all the other essays provide valuable background to the period.

David Scott Kastan *A Companion to Shakespeare* (Blackwell, 1999)
A comprehensive set of essays covering the literary, theatrical, social and intellectual background of the times.

Alexander Leggatt *English Drama: Shakespeare to the Restoration, 1590–1660* (Longman, 1988)
A helpful account of how the period fostered radical experiments in drama.

Russ McDonald, ed. *The Bedford Companion to Shakespeare* (Bedford Books at Merlin Press, 1996)
A valuable collection of contemporary documents presented in context.

R E Pritchard *Shakespeare's England: Life in Elizabethan and Jacobean Times* (Sutton Publishing, 1998)
A clearly written, illustrated account. Very suitable for a first introduction.

Criticism

M C Bradbrook *Shakespeare: the Poet in his World* (Methuen, 1980)
Places Shakespeare in the social and dramatic context of his times.

A C Bradley *Shakespearean Tragedy* (Penguin, 1991; originally published in 1904)
The most important source of 'character criticism'. Although written almost 100 years ago, its clear, conversational style make it still very readable.

H B Charlton *Shakespearean Tragedy* (Methuen, 1948)
A clearly written introduction, mainly concerned with character, but calling for a
synthesis of approaches to the tragedies.

Jonathan Dollimore *Radical Tragedy: Religion, Ideology and Power in the Drama
of Shakespeare and his Contemporaries* (second edition, Harvester Wheatsheaf,
1989)
Dollimore's writing makes many demands on the reader, but his book is an
important landmark in the study of Shakespearean and Jacobean tragedy.

Jonathan Dollimore and Alan Sinfield *Political Shakespeare: New Essays in
Cultural Materialism* (second edition, Manchester University Press, 1994)
The Introduction provides an overview of 'new approaches', and Stephen
Greenblatt's essay 'Invisible bullets' demonstrates the method of new historicism.

Juliet Dusinberre *Shakespeare and the Nature of Women* (second edition,
Macmillan, 1996)
A key text in feminist approaches to Shakespeare. Dusinberre is committed to the
notion that Shakespeare saw women and men as equal. Her Introduction to the
second edition helpfully outlines feminist approaches.

Stephen Greenblatt *Shakespearean Negotiations: the circulation of social energy
in Renaissance England* (Oxford University Press, 1988)
An important but demanding book for those who wish to follow up his essay
'Invisible bullets' in Dollimore and Sinfield above.

Frank Kermode *Shakespeare's Language* (Penguin, 2000)
A detailed examination of how Shakespeare's language changed over the course of
his playwriting career. The chapters on the major tragedies are full of helpful detail.

Victor Kiernan *Eight Tragedies of Shakespeare: a Marxist Study* (Verso, 1996)
Kiernan acknowledges that there are many kinds of Marxist approaches to
Shakespeare. His interpretation of the tragedies singles out particular themes, for
example: the hero, villains and revengers, religion and philosophy.

Jan Kott *Shakespeare Our Contemporary* (second edition, Methuen, 1967)
Kott's interpretations are born out of his experience as a Pole who suffered under
Nazi and Stalinist oppression. Kott's claims that Shakespeare's plays show the
despair that afflicts humankind, and the working out 'the Grand Mechanism' of

history, have had a major impact on scholarship and on productions of Shakespeare.

J W Lever *The Tragedy of State* (Methuen, 1971)
Lever argues that tragedies should be interpreted as about society, rather than about individuals. The reprinted 1987 edition has a valuable introduction by Jonathan Dollimore.

Kiernan Ryan *Shakespeare* (third edition, Macmillan, 2000)
A very clearly written approach that combines traditional interpretations with recent radical approaches.

G. Wilson Knight *The Wheel of Fire: Interpretations of Shakespearean Tragedy* (revised edition, Methuen, 1949)
A vivid example of a metaphysical approach to the tragedies, giving interpretations in terms of symbols and poetic atmosphere; firmly anchored in character criticism.

Films, videos, websites

Videos of the major Shakespearean tragedies are readily available in bookshops and libraries. For some plays (for example, *Hamlet* and *Macbeth*) a number of different versions are available, making it possible to compare different stagings of the same speech or scene. A useful list of Shakespeare films and videos is in Cathy Grant *As You Like It* (British Universities Film and Video Council, 1992). The website BUFVC.ac.uk gives access to updated details through their NISS reference.

A full list of BBC Shakespeare videos can be obtained from BBC Videos for Education and Training, Room A2025, Woodlands, 80 Wood Lane, London W12 0TT. The BBC publication Videos for Education and Training also contains details of *The Duchess of Malfi* and *The Changeling*.

Texts of Shakespeare's tragedies are available on a number of websites for example:
http://www.shakespeare.com
http://www.daphne.palomar.edu/shakespeare

Valuable information about tragedies currently in performance, or background material on the times can be found on:

Royal Shakespeare Company   http://www.rsc.org.uk
Shakespeare's Globe   http://www.shakespeare-globe.org.uk
The Shakespeare Centre   http://www.shakespeare.org.uk

Glossary

Anagnorisis   this Greek word for 'recognition' was used by Aristotle to describe how the hero of a tragedy moves from ignorance to knowledge, coming clearly to recognise what causes his or her suffering.

Aristotle   a Greek philosopher (384–322 BC) whose writings on tragedy in his *Poetics* have had a profound influence on all later dramatic theory.

Blank verse   lines in a play written in unrhymed iambic pentameter (a measure of the rhythm of verse in which each line has five stresses: ti-TUM ti-TUM ti-TUM ti-TUM ti-TUM).

Catharsis   this Greek word meaning 'purgation' was used by Aristotle to describe the effect of tragedy on each member of the audience. Catharsis is the experience of pity and fear which cleanses (purges) the emotions.

Character criticism   interpretations of drama and literature through character analysis. Although character criticism has a long history, it is usually associated with the approach of A C Bradley in his book *Shakespearean Tragedy* (1904).

Chorus   narrator who introduces or comments on the play.

Cultural materialism   an interpretative approach which claims that all forms of culture (e.g. tragedy) are always influenced by material (economic), political and ideological factors. In practice, it is much concerned with how Shakespearean and Jacobean tragedy can be used in criticism of modern society.

Deconstruction   postmodern criticism of various types, for example: taking a play apart to identify its components; claiming that texts have no meaning; identifying contradictions and paradoxes in texts.

Feminist criticism   although there are many kinds of feminist approaches, they all share the intention of showing how female experience is portrayed in literature, drama and criticism (experience that was often neglected or underplayed in traditional criticism).

Genre   types of drama such as tragedy, history, comedy can be described as genres, identifying a group of plays that share key features of form, theme and approach. Because a genre has its own particular conventions, a play in that genre usually arouses specific expectations in an audience.

Hamartia   this Greek word for 'error' was used by Aristotle to describe the 'tragic flaw' which causes the downfall of a tragic hero: some defect of character, error of judgement, ignorance, or human frailty.

Hubris   a Greek word which means excessive pride, or arrogance. It is the tragic flaw which affects some tragic heroes, causing their downfall and death.

Hyperbolic   obviously extravagant and 'over-the-top' language.

Jacobean tragedy   tragedies written during the reign of King James I (1603–1625). *Jacobus* is Latin for James. Tragedies written a few years after this period are conventionally included in this description e.g. John Ford's *'Tis Pity she's a Whore* (c. 1630).

Machiavellianism   deceitful, villainous and crafty behaviour. The term derives from the Italian writer Niccolo Machiavelli (1469–1527) whose book *The Prince* argued that a ruler can use any dishonest and cunning trickery to stay in power.

Malcontent   a character type in Elizabethan and Jacobean tragedy. A discontented man who comments sardonically and cynically on everything and everyone around him. Often an opportunist, wishing to improve his social status. A modern comic malcontent is Rowan Atkinson's portrayal of Edmund Blackadder in the television series *Blackadder*.

New historicism   an interpretative approach which focuses on the Elizabethan and Jacobean period, showing how drama was rooted in the social conditions of the times. It argues that the state tolerated theatre, because the effect of staging plays was to reduce and contain social criticism.

Patriarchy   a social system in which men are in supreme authority and control in the family and in society. Females have little or no power, and are regarded as possessions of the males. Shakespearean and Jacobean tragedies are typically set in patriarchal societies.

Peripeteia   an unexpected reversal of fortune. The main character in tragedy typically experiences a fall from prosperity to suffering and death.

Psychoanalytic criticism   approaches tragedy through character. Its interpretations, influenced by the theories of Sigmund Freud and other psychoanalysts, focus on characters' unconscious desires, sexuality, fantasies and anxieties.

Revenge tragedy   tragedy in which the action arises mainly from the desire of a character to avenge a wrong. Most Shakespearean and Jacobean tragedies contain at least one character seeking revenge.

Rhetoric   in Elizabethan and Jacobean times, rhetoric was the art of persuasion through language. In modern times 'rhetoric' has become a negative label for empty, high-flown, pretentious-sounding language.

Tragicomedy   a mixed genre in which comedy and tragedy are mingled together. All Shakespearean and Jacobean tragedies have elements (sometimes substantial) of comedy.

Tragic flaw   see *hamartia*.

Tragic hero   traditionally this meant the male, upper class character in tragedy who falls from prosperity to suffering and death. Today it is free of both gender and social status and can mean any main character in a tragedy (e.g. Shakespeare's Cleopatra, or Willy Loman in Arthur Miller's *Death of a Salesman*).

Index